Empowering to Improve the World in Sixty Lessons Version 1.0

Fernando M. Reimers

with

Abimbola Adetunji, Alexandra Ball, Christian Bautista, Deaweh Benson, Nicolas Buchbinder, Isabelle Byusa, Wendi Cui, Madhuri Dhariwal, Elaine Ding, Cassie Fuenmayor, Kara Howard, Heather Kesselman, Katherine Kinnaird, Maria Lee, Sharon Jiae Lee, Quinn Lockwood, Xin Miao, Eva Flavia Martinez Orbegozo, Matthew Owens, Theodosia Papazis, Arianna Pattek, Emily Pope, Vijayaragavan Prabakaran, Nicolas Riveros, Ben Searle, Tatiana Sevchenko, Heer Shaikh, Sam (Shiv) Sharma, Chloe Suberville, Somoh Supharukchinda, Corrie Sutherland, Tisha Verma, Devon Wilson, Holing Yip, and Chihiro Yoshida

ISBN-10: 1546456775
ISBN-13: 978-1546456773
Library of Congress Control Number: 2017907482
CreateSpace Independent Publishing Platform
North Charleston, South Carolina

"If we want generations to be good global citizens, it's not enough to teach them writing and reading, but we should instill ethics and human values in their education as well."

Hanan Al-Hroub, Winner Global Teacher Prize 2016

"These sixty lessons show that from the time children step into school until they graduate, they can learn to feel, think and act with the awareness of global citizens, through activities that gradually open their minds onto our interdependence, diversity and shared humanity. By tying in with the 17 Sustainable Development Goals, this curriculum offers practical guidance to nurture a generation of engaged, understanding and committed leaders, motivated by a responsibility to improve human well-being and protect our planet."

Irina Bokova, Director-General of UNESCO

"The most profound part of the mission of an educator is to prepare students to succeed in a diverse and interdependent world. "Empowering Students to Improve the World in Sixty Lessons" is proof that educators are not alone in believing that this work must be intentional, from preschool to graduate school. This book is an important teaching tool that can enlarge the world of our students and focus conversations, self-reflection and imagination toward becoming true problem-solvers, aware that we are all citizens of the same world and that we have a responsibility that requires our collective action if the moral arc of the universe is to bend towards justice, peace and happiness."

Lily Eskelsen Garcia, President, National Education Association

"Fernando and his students set out to write, quite literally, a roadmap to change the world. What resulted is as insightful as it is ambitious and as simple as it is significant—it's an exceptional read for anyone who is looking to find and leverage the transformative power of education."

Jim Ryan, Dean of the Faculty and Charles William Eliot Professor, Harvard Graduate School of Education

"A wonderful resource of high quality, practical and accessible materials enabling schools to achieve the ambitious goal of creating global citizens that understand and value the world and are able to work collaboratively to improve it. This book will help teachers and students view the world from the distant vantage point of space to realize that we are all part of one global community."

Colleen Henning, Head of the Science Department, St. John's College, South Africa

"Recent developments in the global landscape alert us to the dangers of fracturing fault lines across nationalities and societies. The need for global citizenry has never been more urgent. Fernando, with his brilliant team of Harvard scholars, has put together an indispensable curriculum resource for all concerned with building our next generation to be globally-minded. The 13 steps illustrated are cleverly synthesized, simple and yet catalytic."

> Oon-Seng Tan, Director, National Institute of Education-Nanyang Technological University

"I am not an Athenian or a Greek, I am a citizen of the world". Socrates' insights for a sustainable cosmos is skillfully transformed into an inspiring, practical step by step guide, full of imaginative lesson plan ideas, fostering global citizenship education that supports teachers of all curriculum areas and age groups. A must-have, rare tool in the hands of all educators who are determined to enable their students Be the Change the want to see in the world."

> Aggeliki Pappa, Founder, CEO "I Love Dyslexia" EFL school, President 3DlexiaCosmos NPO, Top 10 Finalist Global Teacher Prize 2016

"Fernando Reimers and his students have written a must-read for all educators in all stages of the world. For those who believe in the power of the students, are advancing global citizenship education at your school in order to improve the world, this book is for you."

> Hiroshi Kan Suzuki, Former Minister of State for Education, Japan Ministerial Aide to Japanese Minister of Education, Professor, The University of Tokyo

"Thanks to this book, the dream of global citizenship for my students just became a reality."

> Joe Fatheree, Top 10 Finalist Global Teacher Prize 2016, NEA National Award for Teaching Excellence 2009, Illinois Teacher of the Year 2007

"The book is the guide for teachers to create a school curriculum that is relevant to challenges of the present day. It shows that the best solution for opening schools to the world is teachers cooperation and in the book they propose several useful lessons aligned to the Sustainable Development Goals. Teachers can find five lesson plans per grade to be taught in various subjects with or without modification. In the book there are additional resources for teachers and students, important notes, key questions, links to videos, books and interactive exercises. It helps teachers to bring the world to the classroom to help students understand what global citizenship means. I strongly recommend this book to all teachers as I have found in it lots of valuable guidelines for myself."

Jolanta Okuniewska, Primary School nr 13, Olsztyn, Poland

"Educating global citizens is one of the core challenges of the teaching profession today. "Empowering Students to Improve the World in Sixty Lessons" is not only a great tool to help our teachers educate for global citizenship, it is also a stark reminder that our schools are the only safeguard of our human and democratic values."

Fred van Leeuwen, General Secretary, Education International

"Busy teachers that want to empower their students as global citizens can now easily do so, using the innovative and inspiring lessons here provided. Professor Reimers and his students have done the hard work so we can do the important one: teach. With 5 lessons per grade and a 13-step plan for schools, even novice educators can become global teachers."

Elisa Guerra, Founder & Teacher, Colegio Valle de Filadelfia, México

"From climate change to growing economic inequality, our most urgent problems are global. If we are to successfully confront these challenges, our youth must understand their power as global citizens, and the responsibilities that come with that power. *Empowering Global Citizens* provides teachers with practical tools – curriculum, learning strategies and lesson plans – that they can use in their classrooms to educate their students into 21st century global citizenship."

Randi Weingarten, President, American Federation of Teachers

"This book provides tools to guide teachers, students and the educational community, to develop citizenship competences . The curriculum presented , oriented to empowering global citizens, can help to face many questions that arise from the world`s current political situation. It also helps the reflexion we should be developing about the way we are educating this generation."

Cecilia Maria Velez White, Rector Universidad Jorge Tadeo Lozano and Former Minister of Education, Colombia.

"An urgent call to action for schools to educate for global citizenship, this book provides a comprehensive collection of adaptable lessons for teachers of all grade levels."

> Noah Zeichner, Social Studies Teacher and 2015 Global Teacher Prize Top 50 Finalist Seattle Public Schools

"It is great to see student awareness of natural resources -and specifically plant use - deftly embedded in the effective pedagogical practices of communication and student choice! These lessons superpower students to improve the world by sparking environmental problem solving."

> Naomi Volain. Top 10 Finalist Global Teacher Prize 2015, NASA Network of Educator Astronaut Teachers.

"At a time when global awareness and critical thinking about international issues are more important than ever before, Dr. Reimers has developed an incredible resource. This book provides educators what they need to develop global problem solvers and to help every student see the power in using learning as a way to make the world a better place."

> Michael A. Soskil, Head Teacher Science Wallenpaupack South Elementary, 2017 Pennsylvania Teacher of the Year and 2016 Global Teacher Prize Top 10 Finalist

Table of Contents

Section I: Thirteen Steps to Empowering Students to Improve the World

Fernando M. Reimers

Introduction: Goals of the chapter and of the book

Globalization requires a new emphasis on global citizenship education. This means helping students understand and appreciate human rights and shared global challenges thus becoming engaged citizens. To do this well, purposeful and high quality global citizenship curriculum is essential. To be able to 'create space' for new curriculum, and to support it, schools must develop and implement an intentional strategy of global citizenship education. This book offers three tools to assist student, teachers and school leaders in that process. The first is a protocol to design and adapt global citizenship curriculum. The second is a protocol to design a school wide strategy for global education. The third is an actual curriculum prototype, a sixty lesson global citizenship curriculum, developed following the process presented in the book. In this chapter you will find aprotocol to design global citizenship education curriculum, and the protocol to develop a school wide global citizenship education strategy, a process to support the implementation of this curriculum. The chapter is followed by the actual curriculum, a set of 60 lessons for grades k-12.

The book is addressed primarily to teachers and school and district leaders, interested in creating opportunities for their students to understand the world in which they live, and to learn to improve it. It can also be useful directly to students in elementary and secondary education who may, in some cases, take the initiative to themselves create curriculum or partner with their teachers in creating opportunities for them to learn about globalization in their schools. Parents and others who can support schools in becoming more relevant may also find the book helpful.

This chapter explains what global citizenship and global citizenship education are. I then explain why they are more necessary than ever and why the current challenges to the values of freedom, equality and globalism call for intentional global citizenship education. I then explain the three motivations to write this book and to develop this curriculum. I present the process I have developed for any group of teachers to develop a coherent and rigorous curriculum, followed by a simple thirteen-step framework which will enable any school to design and execute a global citizenship education strategy.

One of the steps in this thirteen steps process involves the development of a prototype, such as a global studies curriculum, much like the 60 lessons presented in this book. Developing such a curriculum is also simple and within the reach of most schools. In this book, we demonstrate how following the process proposed here can produce a coherent global citizenship curriculum. Having a concrete prototype makes it possible to obtain feedback, to have clarity among many different people about what we mean when we say global citizenship education, to try it and to learn from it. I shared this curriculum with a group of highly recognized teachers from several different countries, who wrote generous endorsements for the book, and their views on the potential utility of the curriculum served as a point of validation.

This curriculum will support teachers who teach students, from kindergarten to high school, how to improve the world. The strength of this curriculum is its simplicity. It requires only teaching five lessons in each grade, a task within the reach of most schools. This makes the Sixty Lessons curriculum widely accessible, and potentially scalable. In spite of such simplicity, the curriculum is a rigorous and robust sequence aligned to a clear set of learning outcomes, which are in turn aligned to an ambitious vision to improve the world. The curriculum is aligned to a map of global competencies that characterizes a high school graduate who understands globalization and appreciates the opportunities it offers for people to collaborate, across lines of difference, in improving the communities of which they are a part, from local communities to global communities. These competencies are, in turn, aligned with the Sustainable Development Goals, a compact of seventeen targets intended to create a world which is sustainable and where peace can be lasting (United Nations 2015).

This curriculum was developed with graduate students in my "Education Policy Analysis and Research in Comparative Perspective" course at the Harvard Graduate School of Education. These are students with strong international interests and many have worked overseas, often with grassroots organizations, service programs, or with governments or other agencies. Many of them are interested in working in the field of international development, which is predicated on the notion that human well-being can be enhanced as a result of the choices made by governments and by other institutions that collaborate with them. Their disciplinary backgrounds are diverse: some of them have studied education, political science, economics, international relations, science and other fields. This group of graduate students is also culturally and ethnically diverse; they span multiple nationalities, religious faiths, and races. They are, collectively, a well-traveled group. In sum, they are a significantly more cosmopolitan group than the average college graduate. Through their studies, work, travel and life they have experienced globalization, and can see the possibilities it offers to advance human well-being and to address the global risks we share.

I had three goals in leading this group of students in developing the curriculum:

The **first goal** was to serve a pressing need for high quality instructional materials which can help K-12 teachers **educate for global citizenship**.

The **second goal** was to **prototype an approach to develop global citizenship curriculum** which would be widely accessible.

The **third goal** was **to collaborate with my students** as part of their education.
I explain each of these motivations below as they will help the reader of this book better understand and appreciate the curriculum we are offering.

Goal 1: Educating for global citizenship

What is Global Competency and why it matters.
To be a competent global citizen is to understand the forces bringing the world together at accelerating speed, and to have the capabilities to operate effectively across the boundaries of a single nation state, to address the challenges they create, or to seize the opportunities they afford. However, the capacity of most people to make sense of such global integration is limited. By forces that bring the world together, I mean processes which cross over the boundaries of a single nation state and which cannot be explained or addressed within those boundaries, such as climate change or terrorism. As a result of our inability to understand globalization, we may unwittingly respond to those challenges inadequately and produce dislocations causing human suffering.

Sophistication and competency is especially important to address global challenges because the institutional framework to address them is limited. There is no global jurisdiction in the same way in which there is a national jurisdiction. There is no global passport, global currency, or global language.

While there are indeed numerous global institutions, with explicit responsibilities for global governance, the mechanisms to access them or hold them to account elude most people in ways that national institutions of governance do not.

Sadly, most people have not had the opportunity to develop an educated approach to the critical challenges which affect their lives, or could affect them in the future. The World Economic Forum has, over the last decade, conducted an annual exercise of identifying and analyzing the major global risks. The most recent Global Risk Report identifies five trends affecting major developments as: 1) Rising income and wealth disparity, 2) Changing climate, 3) Increasing polarization of societies, 4) Rising cyber dependency, and 5) Aging population. These trends will in turn lead to significant interconnections among risks such as 1) Unemployment and underemployment, with ensuing social instability, 2) Large scale involuntary migration, and in some cases to state collapse or crisis, 3) Failure to control climate change or adapt to it and water crises, 4) Failure of national governance and social instability, and 5) Interstate conflicts with regional consequences and ensuring large scale migration (World Economic Forum 2016). In order to effectively manage these risks, it is important that people understand them, and that they are capable of responding effectively to them. For example, there is a significant disconnect between the scientific evidence documenting global warming and the knowledge, attitude and behaviors of most people with regards to the options which are possible to slow down global warming. Some even question the evidence, most ignore it, few are ready to change their behaviors in the ways necessary or to assume the costs of slowing down global warming. It is evident from these responses that educational institutions are not adequately preparing people to understand some of the global risks we face, to be disposed to address them or to have the skills to be effective in mitigating such risks.

Addressing some of these global challenges requires global cooperation among individuals and leaders across national boundaries. For instance, climate change is a deterritorialized process as nation states do not enjoy their separate national atmosphere. Climate change has other global multiplier effects. For instance, it can cause people to abandon their homelands because farming is no longer possible, contributing to the growth of megacities. Rapid population growth and urbanization brings with it new challenges, particularly if the rate of job creation does not keep up with urban population growth. This leads to people living in poverty and to social exclusion, with potential to lead to conflict, perhaps in the form of increased common crime, but also political conflict, which can cause people to migrate in large numbers, causing dislocations in the nations to which refugees migrate.

Because the systemic complexity of some global challenges eludes those who have not had the opportunity to learn to understand them, their response to some of these risks and effects of globalization may be to want to withdraw from the process, to isolate themselves from the rest of the world, to go back to a safe place and time, even if that time and place exists only in their mind. Some see jobs disappear in their communities and attribute this to global trade or the migration of capital, rather than to the transformation of economic opportunities resulting from automation. Some attribute their own diminished opportunities to immigration rather to the increased skill requirements of the jobs available. As a result of these perceptions, which are to a great extent unsupported by an evidenced based understanding of these processes, there is a resurgence of a form of nationalism which rejects globalization. This emerging populist nationalism has created veritable divides within many societies, between those who see themselves as part of a global community, with shared responsibility to address some of these challenges, and those who do not see themselves as global citizens. A survey administered by the BBC in a range of countries shows that while the percentage of the population that sees themselves as global citizens is growing over time, there are clear splits in the population in most countries in this respect. There are also important differences across countries. For example, in 2016, when asked whether they agreed with the statement 'I see myself more as a global citizen than a citizen of my country', one in four people in Canada strongly agreed with that statement, and an additional 28% somewhat agreed. On the other hand, one in four people disagreed strongly with the proposition, and an additional 21% somewhat disagreed. The population is, therefore, split in the middle, with half of the population divided between two extreme views. These data are shown below in figure 1. Similar divisions are seen in the United States, with 36% of the population strongly disagreeing with the statement.

Figure 1. Percentage of the population who sees themselves more as global citizens than as citizens of their own country (BBC 2016).

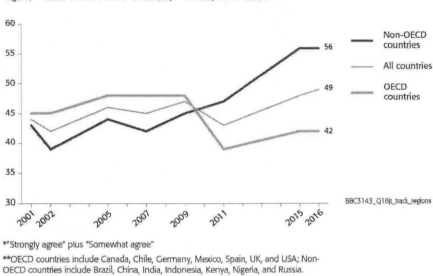

I See Myself More as a Global Citizen than a Citizen of My Country
"Agree,"* OECD vs Non-OECD Countries,** Trends, 2001–2016

*"Strongly agree" plus "Somewhat agree"
**OECD countries include Canada, Chile, Germany, Mexico, Spain, UK, and USA; Non-OECD countries include Brazil, China, India, Indonesia, Kenya, Nigeria, and Russia.
Not all countries were asked in all years.

There are also divides among countries in how these views are changing over time. In the OECD nations participating in the study, the percentage of those who see themselves as global citizens has held relatively steady over time, whereas it has increased in non OECD nations, as seen in figure 2.

Figure 2. Percentage of the population who sees themselves more as global citizens than as citizens of their own country by country (BBC 2016).

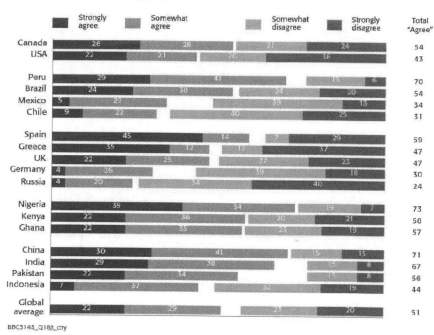

BBC3143_Q18jt_ctry

The white space in this chart represents "Depends, neither agree nor disagree," and "Don't know."

While the global risks identified by the World Economic Forum have the potential to cause harm and suffering, the process of globalization itself, resulting largely from the transformation in communication, organization and production of goods and services and technological developments, is neither good nor bad. Whether such a process improves or diminishes human well-being depends on the uses we make of these elements of globalization. How we value these processes depends also on the criteria we use to judge their outcomes and in how we weigh their various outcomes. For example, technology enabled communications crosses over the boundaries of nation states. The vast integration of computer infrastructure which we know as the internet, allows low cost instantaneous communications among humans, and increasingly among humans and machines, across the globe. The low cost of such communications has extended the opportunity for global communications to a significant percentage of the population. In itself, this is neither good nor bad. The uses to which we put these communications can lead to outcomes that we may deem as positive or negative. The internet can be used to facilitate communications among public health specialists, or to augment their capacity with access to artificial intelligence, advancing human health across the globe. To most of us this is a positive outcome, because we value human life. These collaborations to advance health may now distribute work across people who work in rather different economies, with different standards of living. For example, a hospital in Boston can transmit digital files with x-rays very rapidly to a medical center in the developing world, where they can be interpreted by trained personnel willing to perform work of the same quality for less compensation than the same work performed in Boston. How we value the outcome of this global integration of medical work depends on the weight we assign to the person who gains the opportunity to perform the work and to the person who loses that opportunity, and to the health of the person who benefits from the service because the possible reduction in cost. We might also conclude that such transformation in how goods and services are produced relying on a wider base of global resources, as opposed to resources in a narrowly defined geography is simply efficient and that over time the dislocations caused by the loss of work in one part of the world will be offset as new industries emerge which employ the talents of those out of work, maybe in occupations that add higher value and that require, therefore, higher levels of skills.

Some of these developments characterizing globalization have happened so rapidly that we do not yet appreciate their implications. The forms of human organization which technology-enabled infrastructure has made possible are simply unprecedented in human history. Nearly two billion people, one third of humanity, use the social network Facebook every month, about 1.2 billion of them daily. There are all kinds of good uses that such platform enables. I am able to be in regular communication with the graduates of the graduate program in International Education Policy I direct at Harvard through a Facebook group. These graduates have also self-organized into regional sub-groups, which allow them to access the support of their peers as they perform their professional duties. In this way, Facebook enables a form of 'collective intelligence' that would have been impossible before the internet. Thanks to technological infrastructure, there are many global networks of individuals where it is truly possible for members of each network to benefit from the collective expertise of the network. At the same time, Facebook can and has been abused by groups who organize with the intent of causing harm to others, hate groups for example, or to spread misinformation, creating 'echo chambers' in which 'alternative facts' are given the same credence as the truth.

The emerging and increasing conflicting views between groups in the population regarding globalization brings with it the risk of open social conflict. In its most extreme form, this conflict can lead some to rejecting the basic liberal values which are the foundation of much human progress over the last century. In the United States, for example, the Southern Poverty Law Center has documented an increase in hate groups and hate crimes in recent years (Southern Poverty Law Center 2017).

It is thus that the political philosophy of liberalism, which has oriented much of the work of governments and of the global institutions created after World War II is increasingly challenged by populist and nationalist movements. Given that education, at least in its aspiration to be universal, is a cornerstone of the liberal project, it is necessary that schools make visible the underlying values to the aspiration of extending education to all.

Global Education is at the Core of Education for All

The idea that all persons should be educated is relatively recent. It is primarily a product of the Enlightenment, and as such a product of liberal political thought, of philosophers such as John Locke, Jean Jacques Rousseau, Adam Smith and others. As part of the ideology of liberalism, public education's goals were to promote freedom and equality, as such they were primarily to educate citizens for a liberal political order (Reimers 2014 and Reimers 2015a).

The Global Expansion in public education benefited from the consolidation of nation states and the expansion of liberalism in the 1800s, and again after World War II as a result of the creation of a global architecture to promote the values of freedom and equality, liberal ideas, around the world (Reimers 2017). This architecture included the adoption of the Universal Declaration of Human Rights, the creation of the United Nations, and the extensive forms of international cooperation which accelerated the process of economic and social development throughout the world (Reimers 2015b).

Under liberalism it was assumed that public education could serve democratic political and economic goals with limited tradeoffs between them. Additional goals such as advancing human rights and modernization were also seen as convergent with political and economic goals. For this reason, most governments advancing education as part of liberalism saw limited tradeoffs between these various goals of education: democratic citizenship, increased productivity, human rights and modernization.

The challenges to liberalism from communism and fascism brought alternative goals for public education, challenging the notion that individuals could be free to choose which education to pursue, and emphasizing political and economic goals, as well as downplaying human rights and modernization goals.

The tensions between the soviet block and the democratic world caused some challenges to global institutions with respect to their efforts in education, and this may well be the reason why the tacit education consensus of many of these institutions was more about getting children in schools than about what they should learn in school or about how what they should learn should align with a vision of a good life and a good society. Consensus on those topics is difficult to reach in international institutions and also in societies in which there is much political contestation. This is perhaps the reason the PISA studies, conducted by the OECD so far have focused on domains such as literacy, mathematics and science, and not on domains like civics or global citizenship, it is also arguably the reason multilateral and bilateral banks financing education reforms have seldom addressed questions of curriculum content, and the reason organizations like UNESCO have found it difficult to advance human rights education around the world, even though they were created to do this.

Countries like the United States or Mexico, where there is more political competition, have found it difficult to reach consensus on a vision of a good society and of what education should prepare students to do and how it should prepare them to live. In contrast, nations with limited political competition, such as Singapore or China, have been able to develop coherent and ambitious visions for how the goals of the education system should be aligned with goals of economic and political development, and have been able to align several key components of their education system, such as teacher selection, preparation and support, with those visions.

Given the difficulties which some countries have faced in reaching consensus on the purposes of education, the next best thing left for those governments was to focus on particular competencies, as their goals, without attempting an integrated view of what the sum of these competencies produces, or explicitly describing how those competencies align with a broader narrative of what social progress means. Most countries focus on the basic literacies of language, mathematics and science. Increasingly the competencies under consideration are expanding, not only to other cognitive domains, but to social and emotional domains. Governments and educators now are also interested in character, self-regulation, self-awareness, grit, tolerance or leadership (Reimers and Chung 2016). But, for the most part, those interests are not framed as part of a discussion of how the integration of those capacities will enable people to individually and collectively advance social or economic goals. This is a difficult conversation to have in settings where there is no consensus among elites on which place their country should occupy in a global economy.

In spite of these challenges to developing clear and coherent visions on the purposes of public education, the dominance of liberalism as the organizing principle of the post World War II order, particularly given the support of countries with large economies also committed to liberalism, fueled a set of educational purposes more or less aligned with the ideals of freedom and equality. The fall of the Berlin Wall, the collapse of the Soviet Union and the acceleration of globalization in the last two decades, made these educational aims of liberalism the dominant consensus in most of the world. The report UNESCO commissioned to Jacques Delors in the 1990s on education for the 21st century is a very good example of this consensus proposing that education in the 21st century should be aligned with preparing people for lifelong learning and with four broad sets of aims: learning to know, to do, to be and to live together. The report recognized the specific choices with regards to these goals should reflect a vision for society (UNESCO 1996).

The undergirding rationale of such consensus was that there were limited tradeoffs between alternative education purposes. That the same skills that helped people become productive also helped them engage as citizens. It was assumed that advancing human rights would also advance freedoms as economic, political, social and cultural development converged. It was also assumed that policies that fostered economic development would result in the emergence of cultural values that were supportive of development, and that this would foster more social inclusion and political development, and that there would be multiple reinforcing loops connecting the many facets of development. It was also assumed that globalization would be mutually reinforcing with these processes, and it was expected that, globally, the world would be moving towards convergence in an ever going cycle towards greater freedom, equality, and happiness.

Since the fall of the Berlin wall, the main political challenges to these liberal views have come from populism[1]. Populism posits that ordinary people are exploited by elites and challenges the notion of representative democracy with direct action by the masses. Since direct action by large numbers is impractical, too often populism results in autocratic rule by a leader, communicating directly with the masses, or pretending to do so, unobstructed by intermediary institutions and by the normal division of power and checks and balance of democratic government. Because of this breakdown of normal democratic checks and balances, some political scientists have argued, based on the historical record of the 1920s and 1930s that populism can give rise to fascism, as happened in Europe prior to World War II, in Argentina with Peron or in Spain with Franco (Eatwell 2017).

Modern populists are exploiting the following ideas. The first idea is that globalization, and liberal policies, do not benefit all, and that there are important groups of the population who are left behind, and without hope of seeing their conditions improve. They attribute this to elites that are not accountable to those groups, and to a model of development that fails to envision a role for these groups which are left behind. Populists also exploit and exacerbate cultural divides among the population, including differences in values and worldviews.

In the recent presidential election in the United States, these divisions are between the political establishment, which advanced views of the Hamiltonians and Wilsonians developed after World War II, with the older views of the Jeffersonians and Jacksonians. The Hamiltonians advanced the idea of the United States playing a global leadership role in creating a global liberal order to contain the Soviet Union and advance US interests. The Wilsonians also advanced a global liberal order in terms of values that would reduce global conflict and violence. They promoted human rights, democratic governance and the rule of law. The Jeffersonians believe that minimizing the global role of the United States would reduce costs and risks. Jacksonian populist nationalists, in contrast, focused on advancing equality and dignity of American citizens, and delinking from cosmopolitan enlightenment ideals and the global liberal order (Mead 2017).

---

[1] For an extended discussion of the challenges that populism poses to the liberal institutions of public education, universities and democracy, and to the values of freedom and equality see Fernando Reimers, *One Student at a Time. Leading the Global Education Movement.* 2017.

These views are a challenge to the ideas of a universal project to advance freedom, equality and human rights, which is the liberal project. They are a challenge to the project of globalization and they may be a challenge to the very idea of representative democracy.

The Risks of Populism and how global citizenship education can help.

There are some risks we can expect to emerge from this state of affairs. The first is a risk to the idea of human rights itself. If nationalism is the new organizing force challenging globalism, the notion of ingroup and outgroup will be defined by citizenship, not by membership in humanity. Because one of the consequences of globalization has been migration, migrants will likely be the first target for exclusion. If cultural wars define the politics of education we should expect to see battles over the rights of cultural and ethnic minorities.

A second risk concerns greater difficulties in addressing global challenges. The prospects for collective action diminish as the world moves towards national populism, and the goals of education move away from preparing students to understand global interconnectedness and globalization.

A third risk is a breakdown of the institutions that were created to protect freedom, democracy, the rule of law, public education, basic freedoms. This is the risk that relates to the evolution of populism into fascism.

A fourth risk is the risk of disorder and social conflict. As trust erodes among different groups of people and as trust in institutions, elites and governments declines, this will make the challenge of resolving conflict peacefully and within the rule of law greater.

Those of us who prefer a global liberal order should support a new focus on education for democratic citizenship, including global citizenship. By global liberal order I mean an order built on three simple ideas, the idea that all people have the same rights, the idea that freedom is preferable to un-freedom and the idea that, as members of the same species, we are bound together in our obligation to advance these rights across national borders, and that we should collaborate peacefully in addressing our shared challenges.

This means supporting educators so that schools can advance human rights, educate about shared global challenges, educate for engaged citizenship, focus on dispositions and values as much as skills, and attend to the conditions that make it possible for schools to be effective in achieving these goals. This is what I call global citizenship education.

To a great extent, education was always meant to be cosmopolitan, global education, but this notion was implicit because the expansion of public education was part of a project that was global and widely supported, the project of advancing human rights and freedoms for all. This project is now contested, and for this reason the ethical foundations of global citizenship education need to be pursued intentionally, with greater resolve and effectiveness than ever. In devising more intentional and effective forms of global education, we will be able to mitigate the emerging conflicts that, as I have described, are emerging from the rise of populism, as all students are equipped with a knowledge base and an understanding, that enables more informed dialogue about the process of globalization, and that predisposes all to seeking peaceful resolutions of our differences and collaborative approaches to addressing our shared challenges. The Sustainable Development Goals, a compact adopted at the 70th General Assembly of the United Nations, outlines a vision of the goals we need to achieve in order to secure sustainability and peace. Inherent in that vision is international cooperation, and the achievement of each of the seventeen goals requires that people develop specific competencies. The development of such competencies is the domain of global citizenship education (Reimers and Villegas-Reimers 2015). It is not surprising that one of the Sustainable Development Goals, Goal number 4, is to ensure inclusive and quality education for all and promote lifelong learning, and one of the targets is to advance global citizenship: *"By 2030, ensure that all learners acquire the knowledge and skills needed to promote sustainable development, including, among others, through education for sustainable development and sustainable lifestyles, human rights, gender equality, promotion of a culture of peace and non-violence, global citizenship and appreciation of cultural diversity and of culture's contribution to sustainable development."* (United Nations 2015). Given this need, UNESCO maintains a website monitoring developments to advance this target. There are useful background reports in that site, the site makes evident the need for adequate curriculum materials and programs to support the development of teacher capacities to lead global citizenship education (UNESCO 2017).

Goal 2: Prototyping an approach to developing global citizenship curriculum

My work in the field of global citizenship education developed as an extension of work I had been doing in the field of citizenship education. In

14

understanding that the world was becoming more interdependent, the global sphere became just one of the communities in which people would need to exercise citizenship (Reimers 2006). Greater focus on the domain of global citizenship evidenced that lack of a clear and shared understanding of what it meant made dialogue difficult among those working in the field, which motivated a chapter proposing a clear definition of the components of global citizenship (Reimers 2009). In 2010, I convened a think tank of leaders of thought and practice in the area of global citizenship education, under the auspices of the Advanced Leadership Initiative I co-chair at Harvard University. This think tank became then an annual program of professional development offered by the Harvard Graduate School of Education. This convening provided me a valuable opportunity to understand the work that is been advanced by practitioners in the field, and the challenges they face, and to collaborate with these practitioners in their efforts to deepen this work in their own institutions.

Between 2010-2012 I designed, with assistance of four graduate students, a global citizenship curriculum for a new independent school (the Avenues School). We developed a framework of competencies aligned with the Universal Declaration of Human Rights, the Millennium Development Goals and the World Economic Forum Global Risk Assessment Framework, and developed an entire, coherent and rigorous K-12 interdisciplinary, project based, curriculum, that required devoting an average of eight hours a week, each week, from kindergarten to high school to global studies. We then made this curriculum widely available in the book Empowering Global Citizens using a Creative Commons License, which invited and authorized people to build on this curriculum and to use it as they wished, and distributed it through Amazon at the lowest possible cost, including as a free kindle book (Reimers et al 2016). The publication of Empowering Global Citizens has been well received by many teachers and school and district leaders, and the book is now used as a resource in public and private schools in the United States and abroad. Chinese and Portuguese language editions are currently in preparation, for distribution of the book in China and Brazil.

But the diffusion of the curriculum presented in Empowering Global Citizens also made me aware of some challenges facing schools adopting it. The first is that few schools have the latitude to devote eight hours a week to teach a new subject and to staff this course with dedicated teachers. I realized also that the units we proposed in Empowering Global Citizens called for knowledge that was not always available to the teachers in the school. Also, the length of the book at 422 pages was discouraging to some teachers and students, who saw the subject as attractive, but not as easily within their reach.

In addition, the curriculum in Empowering Global Citizens was presented at the level of 'units,' not lesson plans. While possible lesson plans were sketched, they were not intentionally developed so that teachers would develop their own lessons, based on the units, attending to the characteristics and interests of their own students, and to their own capacities to teach them. The freedom and time to develop lessons in a new subject is, I learned, something that eludes some teachers. Finally, some of those teachers who began to use that curriculum, quickly realized that they had to align other school processes so they would support teaching it, they had to manage communications with key stakeholders, including parents, explaining the goals of this curriculum, they had to manage the introduction of the curriculum with competing priorities in the school, align it with existing elements of global education in the existing curriculum in the school, and attend to the needs of professional development of teachers, and securing instructional resources to implement the curriculum. As I assisted some of those educators in troubleshooting these challenges, I discovered that successful implementation of a global citizenship curriculum required a school-wide strategy of global education. To address this need, I developed a process to help teachers and school leaders design such a strategy, a process that attended to the organizational and structural conditions that are the foundation of teaching an ambitious new curriculum.

This process includes working with a team that leads the efforts in the school, assisting them in developing a vision and a framework of the profile of their globally competent graduate, and auditing existing global education opportunities in the school using the framework. The process is described in a subsequent section in this chapter, a thirteen step sequence that any school can follow to put in place a global citizenship curriculum. That sequence describes a recursive process in which the teachers and leaders in the school launch a global education program, and continuously learn as they implement it, to take this program over time to growing levels of effectiveness. This process is informed by a course I teach on the design of educational innovations, in which students are encouraged to develop a rapid prototype, launch it, learn from it, and in this way continuously improve it.

A key step in the process I devised is to build a global education prototype, an instructional program of some sort. Because I had seen how Empowering Global Citizens activated the imagination of teachers in providing them with a model of what a coherent and ambitious program could look like, I set out then to design an approach which would allow teachers in any school to develop and teach a coherent and rigorous global citizenship curriculum, one which would be better aligned to their particular school context, students, teachers and resources, than the curriculum presented in Empowering Global Citizens might have been. This is different than inserting a few lessons in some grades, and different to 'infusing' global themes in the existing curriculum. There are already lessons and units available for teachers who want to teach some lessons on global themes. Those have existed for some time. An excellent bank of lessons to teach about each of the Sustainable Development Goals is the website The World's Largest Lesson (The World's Largest Lesson 2017).

While valuable, a collection of lessons is not a curriculum. Lessons aligned to content such as each of the SDGs fail to provide students the sustained and recursive engagement with the domain that leads to high and deep levels of understanding and expertise. Most lessons available are structured around topics or offer very short sequences. We need an organizing framework that reflects and supports the developmental process through which school students go from naïve to expert understandings of the key domains in global studies, while developing also along ethical and social domains that are essential to global competency.

The approach I tested with my students was designed to support the creation of a structured sequence of lessons which would enable the students of that curriculum to progressively master higher levels of understanding and expertise, as learning in higher levels built on learning in lower levels of the curriculum. This was the contribution we ha made with Empowering Global Citizens. The goal this time was similar, but creating not a rich separate course, but a set of five lessons per grade which could be taught in various existing subjects of the curriculum. The curriculum that results from adopting this approach is is different from the infusion of global topics in the curriculum in that infusion calls for creating opportunities for the development of global competency within the structure of existing disciplines. The developmental structure that supports global learning therefore is that of the discipline, and there is no visible structure or sequence underlying the global elements of the curriculum. For instance, in engaging with global themes in a language arts curriculum, student learning follows the developmental arc of the language curriculum. There isn't necessarily an intentional developmental arc to build global competency. This is different from designing an intentional developmental arc for global education, in which there is a clear trajectory where learning in any given level builds on previous levels and provides the foundation for subsequent levels. The lessons in that developmentally structured scope and sequence can be embedded in multiple subjects. In the case of sixty lessons, while the five lessons can be embedded into existing subjects of language, or history or science, there is a discernable scope and sequence that links the five lessons to each other, and the five lessons in each grade to those in other grades, in this way helping students global competency progress from foundational level to advanced levels of knowledge and skill. There is thus a global 'curriculum' consisting of sixty lessons, which may or may not be embedded into existing subjects. Each lesson can be viewed from two sides, the same way in which each block in a Rubik cube has six sides, only two or three of which are visible on the external side of the cube at any given time. One side of the lesson is facing a scope and sequence that forms a coherent global studies curriculum. This is the side presented in the sixty lessons in this book. The other side in each lesson faces the structure of the various subjects in which the various lessons can be taught. Looked at it that way, the developmental arc for global education is not visible, but it is still there as the minds of students are not compartmentalized by subjects of disciplines, but make connections across the curriculum.

Working with teachers and school leaders advancing global education in their schools also made visible that there are three interrelated reasons to pursue global education. The first is simply to help students gain competencies in an increasingly important domain for the reasons articulated in the first section of this chapter. The second is that focusing on global competency as a domain opens the door to innovation in teaching and learning at the school level that will support the development of a range of competencies which are relevant in the 21st century, including self-knowledge and self-management and social skills. In this sense, the introduction of a focus on global education in a school opens the door to more intentional examination of the entire curriculum and its goals, and an opportunity to realign those with the development of competencies which are essential in the 21st century. Finally, the process of change management of a global education strategy is an opportunity to transform the organization and management of schools, in ways that are aligned with the demands and forms of organization of the 21st century. In pursuing the thirteen steps described below, schools will therefore be engaging in a practice of renewal of school culture that can transfer well beyond the specific focus of a global curriculum.

The process I developed to guide the design and management of a school-wide strategy of global education, of which the development of curriculum is but one step, is described in a subsequent section in this chapter, a thirteen step sequence of lessons, not of units as we had done in Empowering Global Citizens, that would provide continuous and extended opportunities for students to gain global competency over the course of multiple grades, much in the way in which they develop literacy or mathematical or scientific skills. While the curriculum in Empowering Global Citizenship illustrated what a rigorous sequence of units could look like, the process proposed here will enable any group of teachers to develop or adapt a simpler version of a global citizenship curriculum, something within the reach of the resources and capabilities available to most teachers.

Unlike the focus of Empowering Global Citizens on 'units', the 60 Lessons curriculum in this book focuses on actual lesson plans. I tested this approach to designing a global studies curriculum with a group of my graduate students, and the result of that implementation of the approach is presented in this book. This product should be treated as a prototype. I do not necessarily expect that teachers will teach these lessons as they are presented here, although they could do so, but that they treat this curriculum as a resource to help them design and evolve their own prototype as described in the thirteen step process in this chapter. They might, initially, teach the sixty lesson curriculum as presented in this book, and then make modifications to these lessons. My expectation is that the fact that this curriculum requires teaching only five lessons per grade, will make it easier to be adopted by most teachers. As they teach these lessons, and modify them, this will increase their capacity and confidence, leading some of them to develop additional lessons in the next iteration of this cycle. This is the reason this book is subtitled version 1.0 - to convey the expectation that schools will work with this curriculum as part of a process of continuous development of their own capacity to teach global education. A successful first iteration with the five lessons presented in this book, might lead a teacher to extend those to 10 lessons in a subsequent year, perhaps drawing on the curriculum offered in Empowering Global Citizens for inspiration.

The approach we followed to develop these lessons is very simple. It can be implemented in a one day workshop, or in a series of shorter meetings. It consists of explaining to those developing the lessons how to go from broad goals to student learning outcomes, reaching agreement on those outcomes, and then organizing the group to develop specific lessons for each grade, and then presenting those to the entire group, and iterating based on feedback to increase alignment across grades.

In preparation for the workshop, participants were asked to read the book *Empowering Global Citizens* and to study the competencies we used to design the curriculum presented in that book. Reading the introductory chapter of that book provides the conceptual understanding of the field of global citizenship, and the units illustrate a structured sequence that aligns goals to competencies and competencies to lessons.those lessons. This publication offers this prototype to those of you who want to teach these lessons, change them, make them your own, and use these sixty lessons as part of the thirteen step process of organizing to deliver an effective global citizenship education curriculum in your school.

Participants were asked to prepare for the design workshop reading the Sustainable Development Goals, and the specific targets for this goals, and to identify knowledge, skills and dispositions that school graduates should gain in school and that would make more likely that those goals will be achieved. The goal would not be necessarily that the students learned the SDGs in school, although that may be useful, but rather that they develop the competencies in school that make the achievement of the goals more likely.

Participants were asked to identify some such learning outcomes and to use the taxonomy created by Dr. Benjamin Bloom in order to educate students in higher order thinking processes such as **analyzing** and evaluating concepts, processes, procedures, and principles, rather than just remembering facts.

Participants were also provided with examples of lesson plans aligned to the SDGs or to global themes and asked to study those prior to the workshop. We suggested the following sites:

http://worldslargestlesson.globalgoals.org/
https://sharemylesson.com/grade/elementary-grades-3-5
https://thewaterproject.org/resources/lesson-plans/?gclid=CISg49Wu6s8CFQVehgod4cQGVQ
http://www.discoveryeducation.com/teachers/free-lesson-plans/
http://www.scholastic.com/teachers/lesson-plans/free-lesson-plans
https://sharemylesson.com/partner/peace-corps-world-wise-schools
http://www.curriculum21.com/clearinghouse/

During the workshop, we worked as a whole group discussing the implications of the SDGs for competencies that students could gain in schools and discussed the framework presented in Empowering Global Citizens. We then collectively defined the specific learning outcomes, and sequenced per grade a pathway to achieve such outcomes. Students then subdivided into groups, and each group worked in a lower and in a higher grade, developing initially two prototype lessons for each grade. Those were presented to the entire group and discussed to achieve a shared understanding of what lessons should look like. They then continued to finalize the design of five lessons per grade. Those were then shared with the entire group for feedback. The entire curriculum w as then made available to the entire team, and all were invited to provide specific feedback and to make revisions. After the curriculum was completed, students audited the curriculum with the SDG goals, to identify to what extent those were being addressed by the sixty lessons. The aspiration was to address as many of the specific targets for all the goals as possible, knowing that in this first iteration, some of the goals might receive less attention.

Based on that feedback, students made revisions to those lessons. Once the entire curriculum was assembled, I shared it with a group of highly accomplished teachers from various countries, who had been selected as finalists for a global teacher prize by the Varkey Education Foundation and invited their views. I then provided additional feedback to the students who made further revisions after examining the entire curricular sequence over several months following the workshop. The result is a prototype which can now be tested. This test could involve actually teaching these lessons, or offering those for feedback to a group of teachers interested in teaching it, and have those teachers make adaptations to those lessons, and then teach them. This publication offers this prototype to those of you who want to teach these lessons, change them, make them your own, use these sixty lessons as part of the thirteen step process of organizing to deliver an effective global citizenship education curriculum in your school.

This is the template to design each lesson I offered the design team.

Lesson Plan Template:

Lesson Plan Title:

Designer: Name of team members

Summary and Rationale: Provide an overview of the lesson. Explain how it fits into the entire curriculum.

Grade:

Time Frame: How much time is budgeted for this lesson?

Subjects: What subjects could this lesson be integrated into?

Instructional Goal: What competencies, knowledge, skills, dispositions, do you hope students will gain in this lesson?

Standards: Which SDGs does this lesson help achieve? Which competencies is it helping to gain?

Understanding Goals:

What are some big ideas or enduring understandings from this lesson

Essential questions: What two to four essential questions guide this lesson? These should be aligned with the understandings and stimulate inquiry and discussion. The questions inspire critical thinking. The questions inspire critical thinking and posting them here will serve to remind you to ask these questions.

Student Learning Objectives:

What specifically do you want the students to learn as a result of this lesson? Write objectives as observable and measurable. Include conditions provided for the student (e.g., in a small group, given a number chart), observable skill or behavior (write, say, draw, engage), and criteria to know if the skill was met (80% accuracy or in 4 out of 5 opportunities). Not all learning objectives are appropriate as observable and measurable –such as dispositions, attitudes, thinking processes in socio emotional domains.

Assessment:

Describe assessment tools which could help teachers know whether students have achieved the intended objectives, include checklists, rubrics, tests and quizzes, informal checks for understanding.

Sequence of Activities: List the sequence of events for this lesson. Include an opener (motivator), core events of the lesson and a conclusion. Indicate how students should be grouped and the question or provocation that will guide their work in each event.

Resources for students: List print or online resources that can support students in carrying out the activities.

Resources for teachers: List print or online resources that can help teachers prepare the lesson.

Here is a summary of the approach to developing the curriculum:
1. Organize a multidisciplinary and multi-grade team.
2. The members of this team read a coherent and rigorous global citizenship education such as the one presented in Empowering Global Citizens
3. Identify which broad goals will guide the curriculum design, for instance the SDGs or the Universal Declaration of Human Rights.
4. Develop a competency framework from those goals which defines a globally competent graduate or a global citizen.
5. Identify a series of learning experiences that will help build those competencies.
6. Structure that series of experiences into developmental sequences of coherent strands, blocks. For instance, a series of experiences may constitute a developmental trajectory around civic engagement, another around sustainability.
7. Develop a set of lessons per grade that address segments of those developmental trajectories appropriate to the age of students in that grade.
8. Audit the coherence of the sequence across grades.
9. Audit all the lessons against the competency framework.

Goal 3: Collaborating with my students

I have long thought that education should be aligned with the purpose of empowering people to become architects of their own lives and contributing members of the communities of which they are a part. I see this purpose as aligned with the basic tenets of the global liberal project of advancing freedom and protecting the fundamental equal rights of all persons. Improving the communities of which we are a part involves collaboration, and since those communities are also, and increasingly, global, this involves building the capacities to collaborate across all lines of difference and boundaries. With respect to these goals, much education has too much of a contemplative bias, and not enough of an orientation to action, necessary for improvement of the world. Perhaps the assumption is that contemplation, or understanding, can lead to action. My work on civic education has persuaded me that in order to educate students to improve the world, education needs to develop not just understanding, but the values, the dispositions and the skills that help engage in such improvement (Reimers 2014, Reimers 2015).

From this perspective, there is no better way to learn to improve the world than to engage in improving it. Education should not be conceived simply as preparation now for engaging with the world at some later point in the future. Rather, the act of engaging with the world as part of the education process is what develops the dispositions and the skills that help improve it. This distinction is important for it reflects two very different epistemologies, theories of how we know. One viewpoint, the contemplative one, presumes that knowledge is the result of study that can be disassociated from and precede action. And that knowledgeable action follows the acquisition knowledge. An alternative viewpoint presumes that knowledge is gained from engaging in action, and that it cannot be disassociated from it. There are many forms of learning where the merits of an action oriented approach are widely accepted: learning to ride a bike, to ride a car, to perform experiments in a laboratory, to do carpentry or masonry, to list a few. A certain amount of prior explanation or observation may be helpful, but one is learning only to ride a bike or ride a car when one is doing it. I will admit that there are domains where prior study may be beneficial to subsequent informed action – learning how various chemical substances react with one another before actually beginning to experiment with them in a lab is probably a good idea, and studying anatomy and observing others perform surgeries is probably more efficient, to the patient at least, than learning from trial and error—but there are clearly limits to what can be generalized to an action setting from studying subject matter decontextualized from the practical uses to which such knowledge can be put. These limitations explain why medical schools use virtual reality, or why business schools use the case teaching method, as a way to provide their students simulated experiences that more closely resemble the context in which they will need to practice their skills, than the context that books, lectures and seminars can help them examine. In many fields, education would benefit from achieving a better balance in the direction of engaging students directly in the solution of problems, as a way to prepare them to solve problems.

There is evidence that US universities do not sufficiently engage their students in solving problems, even though students seem to value the opportunity to do so. A study of 30,000 college graduates, conducted by the Gallup organization, asked them to rate how effective they were at their jobs, and how satisfied they were with them. It then examined which aspects of their college experience best correlated with perceived effectiveness and satisfaction. The strongest predictors were faculty support and experiential learning, such as having engaged in a project extending beyond the requirements of a course, having taken a course which engaged them with real world issues, and having had a professor who had challenged students to achieve more than the students thought they could achieve. Students who had had these three experiences in college where, five, ten, fifteen or twenty years later, twelve times more likely to see themselves as good at their job and satisfied with them than those who had not had any of those experiences. Experiential activities were particularly strong predictors of long term effectiveness and satisfaction, even though only a fraction of the students engaged in experiential learning. Only a third of the students had worked on a project that took a semester or more to complete, only 29% had participated in an internship or a job that allowed them to apply what they were learning in the classroom, and only 20% were active in extracurricular activities or organizations while in college. Only 6% of the students reported strong engagement with the prior three sets of experiential engagements (Ray and Kafka, 2014).

These are the reasons I engage my students in solving real problems. In a course I teach on education policy, for example, students consult for education specialists working in international development organizations and do their course assignments helping that person solve a real world issue. In a course I teach on educational innovation, students design the plan for an organization that is going to advance an innovative way to solve an education challenge.

I see value also in engaging students in learning activities which are neither required nor graded, as a way to cultivate their intrinsic motivation or love for learning, or as in this case, their love for problem solving. When most of the educational experience of students is limited to fulfilling prescribed assignments, following rubrics and being graded for their work, this limits the development of intellectual autonomy and self-direction that professionals need.

Following these ideas, the curriculum presented here was produced by a group of students who volunteered to participate in an extracurricular activity, neither required nor graded, done just for the fun of it, out of intellectual curiosity and desire to improve the world. The only consequences that will matter to the group of students that collaborated with me in producing this curriculum, for the sheer desire to learn and to impact the world, will be how this curriculum is actually used by teachers and the feedback we receive from them. I expect those authentic results to have greater formative value for all of us than any grade I could have provided students for this work. The only consequence that matters in the case of this curriculum, is whether we can contribute in the race against the ignorance that endangers the prospects for peace on this planet.

Thirteen steps to Global Citizenship. A process to create space for rigorous global education in the school.

With the publication of Empowering Global Citizens I learned that a global citizenship curriculum, while important, is only one component of a process of transformation a school must follow to advance global education. Other structures and processes need to support the teaching and the improvement of this curriculum. This is particularly the case if this curriculum is to transcend the boundaries of a course or a subject, and require collaboration among teachers, across subjects and across grades. As already mentioned, such transformation may be beneficial to make education relevant, beyond the specific domain of global education, and it may help develop a culture in the school of greater cooperation and effectiveness, that can transcend the specific focus of this curriculum. In other words, transformation of the school organization and culture is necessary to enable a high quality global education curriculum, and the introduction of such a curriculum can in turn support the transformation of the school organization and culture in ways that are supportive of greater school effectiveness and relevance more broadly.

The following thirteen steps are intended to help a school create such a school culture that is supportive of global citizenship education, and with it the context in which a rigorous and ambitious curriculum of global citizenship can be taught. These steps provide a guide to get organized to deliver a whole school approach to global education. This guide is designed to be used to support the development of a global education strategy, an action plan which can advance ambitious whole school efforts in global education.

The **thirteen steps** are:

1. Establish a leadership team. This team will form the guiding coalition that will design and manage the implementation of the whole school global citizenship education strategy.

2. Develop a long term vision. What are the long term outcomes for students, for the school and for the communities that these graduates will influence that inspire this effort?

3. Develop a framework of knowledge, skills and dispositions for graduates of the school that is aligned with the long term vision.

4. Audit existing curriculum in the school in light of the proposed long term vision and global competencies framework.

5. Design a prototype to better align the existing curriculum to the global competencies framework in step 3 (the sixty lessons presented in this book can serve as an initial prototype, or as a sacrificial proposal that leads to the prototype a particular school adopts).

6. Communicate vision, framework and prototype to the extended community in the school, seek feedback and iterate.

7. Decide on a revised prototype to be implemented and develop an implementation plan to execute the global education prototype.

8. Identify resources necessary and available to implement the global education prototype.

9. Develop a framework to monitor implementation of the prototype and obtain formative feedback.

10. Develop a communication strategy to build and maintain support from key stakeholders.

11. Develop a professional development strategy.
12. Execute the prototype with oversight and support of the leadership team.

13.Evaluate the execution of the prototype, adjust as necessary, and go back to step 4.

Step 1. Establish a leadership team. This team will form the guiding coalition that will design and manage the implementation of the whole school global citizenship education strategy.

Getting the right people on this guiding coalition is critical for the success of a whole school program of global education. It is important that this team is broadly representative of various key constituencies in the school, and of various departments. This is the team that will architect the global strategy, aligning a long term vision of success with specific learning outcomes, and with learning opportunities designed to support students in developing global competency. This team will keep the focus on the strategy, monitor execution of the strategy, troubleshoot the implementation of the strategy in real time, identify necessary support, secure resources and lead the necessary revisions and course-corrections. This team will construct and role model a learning mindset, supporting the development of a school culture that is aligned with the long term vision of success.

Exercise:
Write down the key stakeholder groups critical for a global education strategy in your school? Identify for each group, how are they positioned relative to global education? How much influence do they have? What are their key interests?
Write down the names of the people you think should form the guiding coalition? For each one of them, why are they important? What do they contribute to the process of steering a global education strategy? Map the relationships between members of the coalition and key stakeholder groups?
Prioritize 7-10 members from that group, they will form the guiding coalition.

Step 2. Develop a long term vision. What are the long term outcomes for students, for the school and for the communities that these graduates will influence that inspire this effort?
Write down a long term vision that inspires the global education effort in your school? In the development of the curriculum presented in 'Empowering Global Citizens' (Reimers et al 2016) we used three key frameworks to represent that long term vision: the Universal Declaration of Human Rights, the Sustainable Development Goals, and the Global Risk Assessment Framework of the World Economic Forum. In the development of the curriculum presented in 'Empowering Students to Improve the World in Sixty Lessons' we used the Sustainable Development Goals. For each goal, we identified the student competencies that would help achieve that goal.

Step 3. Develop a framework of knowledge, skills and dispositions for graduates of the school that is aligned with the long term vision from step 2. Examine alignment between those competencies and expected long term goals.

Select a specific group of skills, competencies, knowledge, dispositions, that represent a graduate of the school, which will be used to backward map the curriculum. Examine each of the long term goals against the specific capacities that you seek to help graduates develop. Are they necessary and sufficient? If necessary, revise the expected capacities, going back and forth between competencies and long term goals.

For the curriculum in *Empowering Global Citizens* we developed the following framework of competencies, encompassing intercultural competency, ethical orientation, knowledge and skills, and work and mind habits:

1. Intercultural competency

This includes the ability to interact successfully with people from different cultural identities and origins. It encompasses interpersonal skills as well as intrapersonal skills and ways to govern oneself in the face of cultural differences.

- Interpersonal Skills:
  - Work productively in and effectively lead intercultural teams, including teams distributed in various geographies through the use of telecommunication technologies.
  - Demonstrate empathy toward other people from different cultural origins.
  - Demonstrate courtesy and norms of interaction appropriate to various cultural settings.
  - Resolve culturally based disagreements through negotiation, mediation, and conflict resolution.

- Intrapersonal Skills:
  - Curiosity about global affairs and world cultures
  - The ability to recognize and weigh diverse cultural perspectives
  - An understanding of one's own identity, of others' identities, of how other cultures shape their own and others' identities, and of where one is in space and time
  - The ability to recognize and examine assumptions when engaging with cultural differences

o The recognition of cultural (civilizational, religious, or ethnic) prejudice and the ability to minimize its effects in intergroup dynamics

o An understanding and appreciation of cultural variation in basic norms of interaction, the ability to be courteous, and the ability to find and learn about norms appropriate in specific settings and types of interaction

2. Ethical orientation
- Appreciation of ethical frameworks in diverse religious systems
- Commitment to basic equality of all people
- Recognition of common values and common humanity across civilizational streams
- Appreciation of the potential of every person regardless of socioeconomic circumstances or cultural origin
- Appreciation of the role of global compacts such as the Universal Declaration of Human Rights in guiding global governance
- Commitment to supporting universal human rights, to reducing global poverty, to promoting peace, and to promoting sustainable forms of human-environmental interaction
- Ability to interact with people from diverse cultural backgrounds while demonstrating humility, respect, reciprocity, and integrity
- An understanding of the role of trust in sustaining human interaction as well as global institutions and recognition of forms of breakdowns in trust and institutional corruption and its causes.

3. Knowledge and skills
In addition to highlighting the cosmopolitan links infused in the curriculum, as Kandel recommended a century ago, a global education curriculum should provide students with the knowledge and skills necessary to understand the various vectors of globalization. These include culture, religion, history and geography, politics and government, economics, science, technology and innovation, public health, and demography.
- Culture, religion, and history and geography:
  o World history and geography, with attention to the role of globalization in cultural change
  o The study of religions as powerful institutions organizing human activity
  o Historical knowledge, which includes various perspectives and an understanding of the role of ordinary citizens in history

- o World geography, including the different areas of the world, what unites them, what differences exist, and how humans have changed the geography of the planet
- o World religions, history, and points of contact between civilizations over time
- o Major philosophical traditions and points of connection
- o Performing and visual arts (e.g., theater, dance, music, visual arts, etc.) as a means to find common humanity
- o Different arts and ability to see connections
- o Ability to view art as expression, to use art for expression, and to understand globalization and art

- Politics and government:
  - o Comparative government
  - o How governments work in different societies
  - o Major international institutions and their role in shaping global affairs
  - o Contemporary global challenges in human-environmental interaction
  - o Sources of these challenges, options to address them, and the role of global institutions in addressing these challenges
  - o History of contemporary global conflicts and the role of global institutions in addressing these challenges

- Economics, business, and entrepreneurship:
  - o Theories of economic development and how they explain the various stages in economic development of nations, poverty, and inequality
  - o Institutions that regulate global trade and work to promote international development
  - o Contemporary literature on the effectiveness and limitations of those institutions
  - o The impact of global trade
  - o The consequences of global poverty and the agency of the poor
  - o The demography and factors influencing demographic trends and their implications for global change

- Science, technology and innovation, and globalization
- Public Health, population, and demography

4. Work and mind habits

- Demonstrate innovation and creativity in contributing to formulating solutions to global challenges and to seizing global opportunities; seek and identify the best global practices; and transfer them across geographic, disciplinary, and professional contexts
- Identify different cultural perspectives through which to think about problems
- Understand the process of cultural change and that there is individual variation within cultural groups
- Carry out research projects independently
- Present results of independent research in writing, orally, and using media

Step 4. Audit existing curriculum in the school in light of the proposed long term vision and global competencies framework.

Using the framework of expected competencies for a graduate, identify where in the curriculum –broadly construed, to include curricular, co-curricular and extracurricular activities—are there at present opportunities for students to develop such capacities. The goal of this activity is to identify what elements of a strategy of global education are already in place in the school and can be built upon, and also to identify existing gaps and areas of opportunity to increase the coherence and synergies between the opportunities already available.

This exercise should clearly identify whether there are opportunities to gain such capacities, and whether the same opportunities are available to all students in the school or only to a subset of the students. Are they requirements or electives?

Step 5. Design a prototype to better align existing curriculum to the global competencies framework.

There are multiple ways to initiate a process of global education in a school, and what makes most sense in each case should be based on what is already in place (identified in the audit) and on local conditions, resources and areas of strength. The initiative designed should build on existing strengths but also challenge the guiding coalition to significantly advance the school towards greater ambition, coherence and depth in the opportunities for students to gain global competencies. Examples of such prototype could include a set of lessons for each grade (as in the case of the sixty lessons presented in this book), or a series of projects in each grade, leading to a capstone per grade, aligned to the profile of the graduate and structured in a way that is coherent across grades.

Step 6. Communicate vision, framework and prototype to the extended community in the school, seek feedback and iterate.
The prototype developed in step 5 is only a concept to elicit feedback and suggestions from a wider group of faculty, those who will be involved in executing the strategy –which would likely extend outside the members of the guiding coalition. In his seminal work on change management, former Harvard Business School Professor Jim Kotter underscores that most change efforts in organizations fail because they under-communicate by a factor of ten (Kotter 1995).

Step 7. Decide on a revised prototype to be implemented and develop an implementation plan to execute the global education prototype.
The feedback and suggestions obtained in step 6 should be processed and used to develop a revised version of the prototype, which could constitute the program to be implemented in year 1. This program should be translated into a project management chart, with key milestones, deliverables and individuals responsible.

Step 8. Identify resources necessary and available to implement the global education prototype.
What resources are necessary to execute the prototype? This includes instructional resources, resources to support students, to support the development of capacity of the faculty. In identifying such necessary resources, the guiding coalition will also map available resources, a likely source of resources include parents and institutions in the community.

Step 9. Develop a framework to monitor implementation of the prototype and obtain formative feedback.
The implementation strategy should be used to identify a small set of indicators that will help the guiding coalition keep track of execution, continuously learn from the process of implementation, help identify and troubleshoot problems as they arise, and provide necessary support to the individuals responsible for the achievement of specific tasks.

Step 10. Develop a communication strategy to build and maintain support from key stakeholders.
Implementation of the strategy is, to a great extent, about continuous communication. This is a core responsibility of the guiding coalition, to devise

and execute a communication strategy that allows all key stakeholders to understand with clarity the intended goals, and what success looks like, and that helps them know how they can support the implementation of the strategy.

Step 11. Develop a professional development strategy.

If the prototype is sufficiently ambitious, as it should be, it is likely to require professional development for faculty so they can adequately support students in gaining global competencies. How will they be supported? The guiding coalition should devise a plan that provides ongoing support for professional development. Much of this support should be available in real time, and be school based, and should combine team based professional development, with individual study and coaching. The guiding coalition may consider developing partnerships with other schools and with external organizations, to augment their capacity for professional development.

Step 12. Execute the prototype with oversight and support of the leadership team.

Execution of the prototype should be approached with a learning mindset, understanding that the goal is to improve the strategy. It is essential that the leadership team creates a culture that encourages risk taking, experimentation, and open communication among all teachers and key stakeholders involved in implementation.

During execution the leadership team will oversee the process depending on the monitoring system, provide support as necessary and manage the communication strategy. They should meet periodically to assess implementation, provide formative feedback and make any necessary adjustments.

Step 13. Evaluate the execution of the prototype, adjust as necessary, and go back to step 4.

Once a first cycle of implementation of the prototype has been completed, the leadership team will take stock of what has been learned, systematically obtain formative feedback from all teachers and students involved in implementing it, assess any student work and student views that can help discern the results of the prototype and make any necessary revisions to develop a revised version, or to extend the prototype in new directions, for instance, the five lessons per grade curriculum presented in 'Empowering Students to Improve the World in Sixty Lessons' can be augmented to 10 lessons per grade.

Conclusion

In this chapter, I have described why the current challenges to the values of freedom, equality and globalism call for intentional global citizenship education. Such education is within reach of all schools. A simple thirteen-step process can allow any school to design and execute a process of intentionally educating global students. A step in this process involves the development of a prototype, such as a global studies curriculum. Developing such a curriculum is also simple and within the reach of most schools.

In this book, we demonstrate how following the process proposed here can produce a coherent curriculum. A sixty-lesson curriculum designed to help students develop competencies that can move us closer to achieving the sustainable development goals. It took the disciplined work of 37 graduate students one Saturday to develop this prototype, and some additional hours of revision. This curriculum is clearly far from perfect - no curriculum is. What is most important is that it gives clear direction to take the next step, to try it out and revise it. I am confident that these 37 students will take an active role in promoting the diffusion, utilization and revision of these sixty lessons. As other educators accept the invitation we are extending, I invite you to co-construct with us more and more effective opportunities for our students to learn to improve the world. As they engage in improving it, we will be moving in the direction of a world which is sustainable, inclusive and where we can all live in peace. We don't have forever to do this. Let's press on.

References

BBC. Global Citizenship a growing sentiment among citizens of emerging economies: Global Poll. April 2016.
http://www.globescan.com/images/images/pressreleases/BBC2016-Identity/BBC_GlobeScan_Identity_Season_Press_Release_April%2026.pdf

Roger Eatwell "Populism and Fascism" in Cristobal Rovira Kaltwasser, Paul Taggart, Paulina Ochoa Espejo, and Pierre Ostiguy (Eds.) *Oxford Handbook on Populism*. (Oxford: Oxford University Press. 2017).

John P. Kotter *Leading Change: Why Transformation Efforts Fail*. Harvard Business Review, March-April, 1995, Vol.73(2), p.59(9)

Walter Russell Mead "The Jacksonian Revolt. American Populism and the Liberal Order" Foreign Affairs. March/April 2017.

Julie Ray and Stephanie Kafka "Life in College Matters for Life After College". 2014. http://www.gallup.com/poll/168848/life-college-matters-life-college.aspx

Fernando Reimers "Citizenship, Identity and Education. Examining the Public Purposes of Schools in an Age of Globalization" *Prospects*. Vol 36(3). September 2006.

Fernando Reimers "Leading for Global Competency," *Education Leadership* September 2009. Vol 67 (1).

Fernando Reimers, *The Three A's of Global Education*. (London: Oxfam, 2010).

Fernando Reimers, "Educating for Global Competency" In Joel E. Cohen. and Martin B. Malin (Eds.), *International Perspectives on the Goals of Universal Basic and Secondary Education*. (New York: Routledge Press, 2010).

Fernando Reimers, "Education for Improvement: Citizenship in the Global Public Sphere," *Harvard International Review*, Summer (2013): 56–61.

Fernando Reimers, *Bringing Global Education to the Core of the Undergraduate Curriculum*. Diversity and Democracy. Spring 2014. American Association of Colleges and Universities.

Fernando Reimers, 2015a "Making Democracy Work: A Civic Lesson for the Twenty-First Century" In Dan Eshet and Michael Feldberg (Eds.), *Washington's Rebuke to Bigotry: Reflections on Our First President Famous 1790 Letter to the Hebrew Congregation in Newport, Rhode Island*. (Brookline: Facing History and Ourselves National Foundation, Inc., 2015).

Fernando Reimers, 2015b "Educating the children of the poor: A paradoxical global movement" In William Tierney (Ed). *Rethinking Education and Poverty*. (Baltimore: Johns Hopkins University Press. 2015).

Fernando Reimers and Eleonora Villegas-Reimers, "Taking Action on Global Education," (UNESCO Bangkok Office News, 2015.) http://www.unescobkk.org/education/news/article/taking-action-on-global-education/.

Fernando Reimers and Connie K. Chung. *Teaching and Learning in the Twenty First Century*. (Cambridge. Harvard Education Press, 2016).

Fernando Reimers, Vidur Chopra, Connie K. Chung, Julia Higdon, and E. B. O'Donnell. *Empowering Global Citizens. A World Course* (South Carolina: Create Space. 2016).

Fernando Reimers, (ed). *Empowering All Students At Scale.* (South Carolina: Create Space. 2017).

Fernando Reimers, *One Student at a Time. Leading the Global Education Movement* (South Carolina: Create Space. 2017).

Southern Poverty Law Center. Hate Map. https://www.splcenter.org/hate-map Accessed May 5, 2017.

The World's Largest Lesson. http://worldslargestlesson.globalgoals.org/ Accessed May 5, 2017.

UNESCO. *Learning the Treasure Within. Report to UNESCO of the International Commission on Education for the 21st Century.* (Paris: UNESCO Publishing. 1996).

UNESCO. *Learning to Live Together. Trends and Progress.* 2017. http://en.unesco.org/gced/sdg47progress

United Nations. 2015. Sustainable Development Goals. http://www.un.org/sustainabledevelopment/ Accessed May 5, 2017.

World Economic Forum. *Global Risks Report 2017.* https://www.weforum.org/reports/the-global-risks-report-2017 Accesssed May 5, 2017.

Section II: Goals for the Curriculum

As a result of following the process described in the previous chapter, the following competencies, which we strive to address in 60 lessons, were identified as critical to the achievement of each of the 17 sustainable development goals which are described in detail on the official website at https://sustainabledevelopment.un.org/.

Goal 1. No Poverty

The five specific targets for this goal focus on eradicating extreme poverty, reducing poverty incidence, establishing social protection systems, increasing equity in rights to economic resources and basic services, strengthen the resiliency of the poor, and ensure mobilization of resources to support poverty reduction programs.

The competencies that would be aligned with that goal are those that build the capacities for critical thinking, life skills, lifelong learning and resiliency for the children of the poor themselves, and those that develop the sensibilities of non-poor children to advance opportunities for the poor. For all children, a study of the structural conditions which underlie poverty and the development of respect for human rights of all people, will give them the foundational knowledge and dispositions necessary to work to eradicate poverty.

Goal 2. Zero Hunger

The eight specific targets for this goal focus on eliminating hunger, malnutrition, increasing agricultural productivity, especially of small scale producers, ensuring sustainable food production systems, and supporting rural development and fair trade.

As with the previous goal, this curriculum, in helping the children of the poor develop competencies to get out of poverty, will contribute to the achievement of the zero hunger goal. The curriculum will also develop the sensibilities and skills for graduates of this course to effectively advocate to end hunger.

Goal 3. Good Health and Well Being

The thirteen specific targets under this goal focus on promoting health for women and men. This curriculum, with a strong focus on gender equity, will prepare graduates to support gender equitable policies that will support the good health of women and children.

The competencies prioritized in this curriculum did not specifically target knowledge and dispositions that would support health, although in general the development of critical thinking skills and the capacity to learn to learn will likely support graduates of this course in becoming effective promoters of their own health. The course also develops awareness of the importance of health and cultivates advocates for health for all.

Goal 4. Education

The seven specific targets of this goal focus on universal completion of primary and secondary education leading to relevant learning outcomes, access to quality early child development, gender parity in access to technical and higher education, increase in the number of graduates with technical skills, eliminating gender disparities in education, universal literacy and numeracy and competencies aligned with sustainable development and global citizenship.

The competencies selected in the framework are directly aligned to all of those targets, especially an education for sustainable development and global citizenship, and development of the dispositions and skills to eliminate gender disparities.

Goal 5. Gender Equality

The nine specific targets for this goal focus on eliminating gender discrimination and violence against women, and ensuring full and equal participation of women in society. The competencies selected will empower women to advance their own opportunities, by cultivating their critical thinking skills, capacity to communicate, organize and solve challenges, and their own aspirations for gender equality. The focus of the curriculum on gender equity will also cultivate similar aspirations among male students.

Goal 6. Clean Water and Sanitation

The eight specific targets to achieve universal and safe access to water are not a particular focus of this curriculum though a lesson exploring the origins of our food loosely relates to this topic.

Goal 7. Affordable and Clean Energy

The five specific targets for this goal focusing on access to clean energy are not a focus of the curriculum, although the competencies embedded in this curriculum which promote a value for equality and which foster innovation support these targets.

Goal 8. Decent Work and Economic Growth

The ten specific targets for this goal are addressed in the competency framework in that they will help students develop competencies that will contribute to economic innovation and to productivity, and hence to economic growth and employment. In addition, the focus of the curriculum on human rights, community members and their professions, and the students' own place in the world of work undergirds the targets of fostering innovation and creativity.

Goal 9. Industry, Innovation and Infrastructure

The eight targets of this goal are addressed insofar as the curriculum will promote innovative and entrepreneurial skills in students. The targets pertaining to the development of an industrial infrastructure are not directly addressed in the curriculum.

Goal 10. Reduced Inequalities

The ten targets which this goal encompasses will be addressed as the competencies cultivated by this curriculum will promote increased productivity and employability of the children of the poor and develop the dispositions for all to support pro poor policies, and the economic inclusion of the poor, which reduce inequality. The competencies framework addresses cultural understanding and ethnic diversity, and encourages students to accept the basic equality of all people and their potential. The focus of the curriculum in supporting the development of empowered students who can create change will help advance actions aligned with this goal. A focus of the curriculum is to educate students to question existing power structures and explore community leaders as agents of change.

Goal 11. Sustainable Cities and Communities

The ten specific targets included in this goal pertaining to the development of an urban infrastructure are not directly addressed by the curriculum, although the competencies include the development of environmental awareness and the development of an action orientation which will contribute to sustainable cities. A heavy focus on students as active member of their communities raises awareness of the world around them.

Goal 12. Responsible Consumption and Production

The eleven targets for this goal, related to the development of sustainable consumption and production are addressed by the framework in that students are made aware of the scarcity of water, energy and food, and are taught to analyze and research solutions to problems, including those pertaining to water, energy and food. An explicit focus is the development of responsible consumption of natural resources and the understanding of the food production cycles.

Goal 13. Climate Action

The five specific targets for this goal on the adoption climate change measures are not directly addressed in the curriculum, however the competencies developed by this curriculum will prepare students to respect and understand scientific evidence, in ways that will make it more likely that they will be persuaded to support climate action measures. The competencies developed by the framework will also develop the appreciation for the need of cross-national cooperation in addressing challenges such as climate change.

Goal 14. Life Below Water

The ten targets that stem from this goal to protect life under water are not directly addressed by this curriculum.

Goal 15. Life on Land

The ten targets pertaining to life on land are not directly addressed by the curriculum.

Goal 16. Peace, Justice, and Strong Institutions

The ten targets included in this goal, focused on the reduction of violence, end of exploitation and trafficking and promoting the rule of law will be supported as the curriculum develops an understanding for and an appreciation for human rights. Graduates will understand the importance of legal frameworks and institutions that protect the rule of law.

Goal 17. Partnerships for the Goals

The twenty targets stemming from this goal are indirectly supported insofar as the curriculum develops an appreciation for the importance of international cooperation, and an understanding of the UN system and allied institutions in advancing development.

Section III - Grade-Wise Framework

This section contains 60 lessons, 5 per grade covering grades 1- 12. Each lesson sequence starts each grade begin with an overview which outlines the Learning goal, lesson scaffold. It starts with an overview of the learning goals for each grade it then goes in depth with each lesson.

,

Grade 1

Overview	
Learning Goal	
Learners will understand that they are active members of their community; family, class, neighborhood, and world.	
Lesson Scaffold	
Lesson 1	Who am I? What makes me happy and healthy?
Lesson 2	What is a community? Exploring my class, my neighborhood, my country.
Lesson 3	What happens when we aren't all becoming happy and healthy?
Lesson 4	Equality and Fairness: We are all connected.
Lesson 5	Our very own Declaration of Human Rights.
Learning Objectives	

- Students will cultivate an appreciation and respect for cultural diversity.
- Students will apply concepts learned in class to their community and day-to-day lives.
- Students will think about what they can do to contribute to their own community.

Grade 1 Lesson 1

"Who Am I? What Makes Me Happy and Healthy?"

Time Frame: 60 minutes | **Subjects:** Art, Writing |
Designer: Katherine Kinnaird
Standards: Good Health and Well-Being (SDG 3), Quality Education (SDG 4)

Summary and Rationale: This lesson aims to provide students with a foundation in self-expression and self-awareness so that they will have the tools to think about others in subsequent lessons. It is the first step in students' process of situating themselves in the world.

Instructional Goal: Students will:
- Develop a sense of self-awareness and self-appreciation
- Think critically about what makes them themselves
- Acquire tools for self-expression (written and oral)
- Improve writing and spatial awareness skills through art

Understanding: Building off students' natural curiosity, students will understand what makes them unique, identify their likes and dislikes, and begin to think critically about why they do the things they do.

Essential Questions:
- Who am I?
- What is important to me? Why?
- What do I like to do? What do I dislike? Why?
- What do I want to be in the future? Why?

Student Learning Objectives (Students Will be Able To):
- Tell others about themselves
- Express themselves through both art and writing

Assessment: The teacher can ask students questions throughout the lesson to check for comprehension. The teacher can do this during the opening activity, main activity, and closing activity (see below). Teachers can evaluate students' self-expression using the following rubric:

1 - Limited expression: Students share little or no information about themselves.

2 - Some expression: Students share some information, but provide inconsistent answers.

3 - Adequate expression: Students share information about themselves, their families, their friends, and their likes and dislikes, but do not explain any of their answers.

4 - Good expression: Students share information about themselves, their families, their friends, and their likes and dislikes with the teacher, but not with their classmates.

5 - Excellent expression: Students share information about themselves, their families, their friends, and their likes and dislikes in great detail with the teacher and their classmates.

Sequence of Activities:

- **Opening Activity (10 Minutes):** The teacher prepares students to discuss themselves by reading through a list of activities. Students raise their hand if they like that activity. The teacher selects two students who raised their hands to explain why they like the activity and two children who did not raise their hands to explain why the do not like the activity.
- **Main Activity (30 Minutes):** Students will create a painting of themselves that reflects who or what makes them who they are.
- **Closing Activity (10 Minutes):** Students will then share their painting with the class to build their communication skills.

Resources for Students:

Depending on the class, context, and students' abilities, the teacher can decide whether to show students examples of others' self-portraits (e.g. famous artists' self-portraits or other first graders' self-portraits) or allow students to design their self-portraits on their own.

Resources for Teachers:
Teacher Workshop: Self Portraits: http://tiny.cc/G1L1R1
Primary Portrait Project: http://tiny.cc/G1L1R2
First Grade Self Portraits: http://tiny.cc/G1L1R3

Grade 1 Lesson 2

"What is a Community: My Family, My Class, My Neighborhood"

Time Frame: 60 minutes | **Subjects:** Visual and Performing Art |
Designer: Tatiana Shevchenko
Standards: Decent Work and Economic Growth (SDG 8), Industry, Innovation, and Infrastructure (SDG 9), Reduce Inequalities (SDG 10), Sustainable Cities and Communities (SDG 11)

Summary and Rationale: Students will continue to situate themselves in their community by exploring themselves in the context of the world around them. Students will use visual and performing arts to depict the different roles of the people in their lives.

Instructional goals, students will:
- Learn about the communities they live in and the people who make up their communities.
- Understand the interconnectedness and interdependence of all people in the community
- Develop understanding and respect for different professions within their community.
- Recognize the diverse types of work done at home, at school and outside of these places.

Understanding: Students will understand that their world consists of many different people with many different roles and that the people in their lives are interconnected and interdependent and therefore must be cherished and respected.

Essential Questions:
- Who are the people in my life?
- What role do they play?
- How are the people in our community interconnected?
- How is my daily routine dependent on/connected with my community?
- What would happen if those people stopped doing their community roles?
- How do we show appreciation for the people in our community?

Student Learning Objectives, Students Will be Able To:
- Think analytically about themselves and the different people in their lives.
- Share stories and compare experiences
- Work in teams to create skits
- Perform in front of the class
- Compare and contrast experiences
- Identify different roles and responsibilities of community members around them

Assessments: Students will be assessed based on their level of participation in the activity.

3 Active Participation	2 Moderate Participation:	1 Passive Participation
Student communicates clearly, works well with others, contributes to course discussion and his/her team, participates in the play production and performance	Student actively listens but doesn't share, works with others, participates in the class discussion, has a role in the play but does not contribute to the play's design	Student does not listen or share with others, student does not communicate with his/her team, student does not perform or participate in the production of the play.

Sequence of Activities:

- **Part 1: 10 minutes - Sharing and Mapping**

Teacher and student sit in a discussion circle
Teacher asks students: "*What are the things that you do every day?*"
Students share their answers: ex "I eat breakfast, I ride the bus, I put on my clothes, I go to school etc."

Teacher asks students to expand on their answers ex. "*who helps you with these things, where do the items you use for your daily routines come from, who do you interact with on a daily basis*"
The students answer: ex: "My mom makes breakfast in the morning, my teacher teaches me, my clothes are made by my grandmother/I buy my clothes at the store, the bus driver drives me to school etc."

- **Part 2: 40 minutes - Role Playing**

  - **2.1 : 10 minutes of group work**

Students are grouped into small teams of 2-3. Each member of the team shares his or her scenario from a daily routine and what it would look like without the key community members who are involved in this routine. Members act out what the routine would look like without the key people in their lives, or the key items or tasks which are done by different people in the community. Each group picks one scenario to act out.

Example of a role play:
Setting: Small Town, Morning

> *Student 1 (Role: Student):* I am ready to go to school, I am heading to the bus stop and
>> it's a beautiful day. I take the bus to school every morning, it's great!
>> *Student 2 (Role: Bus driver):* I drive the bus every morning, but today I am sick. I will not be able to drive all the kids to school.
>> *Student 1 (Role: Student):* I am waiting for the bus, but it is not here. I don't think I will be able to go to school today.
>> *Student 3: (Role: Teacher):* I am so worried about my students, I hope they are ok. Nobody came to class today.
>> *Student 1 (Role:Student):* Today was my favorite class, we were going to learn about turtles, but I will not be able to do that. I hope the bus driver is ok!
>> *Student 2: (Role: Bus driver):* I love driving the neighborhood kids to school, I can't wait to go back to work tomorrow so they can go to their lessons and learn many great things.

2.2: 30 minutes - skit presentations

Groups of 3 students (10 groups total based on 30 student class occupancy) act out their
> plays.

- **Part 3: 10 minutes - Discussion**

  After each group has performed their skit the teacher asks students some follow up discussion questions. The teacher will then explain that we will talk about people in our community who help us.

  - What kinds of things do we do every day?
  - Who were the key community members in the skits that we saw?
  - What kinds of jobs, tools, and uniforms do these community members use?
  - What kind of connections do we have among us and with different community members?
  - What would happen if some community members were no longer a part of our community?
  - What are some similarities and differences which we see in our communities and in our daily routines?
  - How do we appreciate our community members every day?

Resources for Students:
*Resources for students are context dependent and assume access to internet and understanding of the English Language

- (Video) Community Discussion by Kids: http://tiny.cc/G1L2R1
- (Video) What Makes a Community: http://tiny.cc/G1L2R2

Resources for Teachers:
- Neighborhood and Communities Around the World: http://tiny.cc/G1L2R3
- A Community is a Place Where People Live: http://tiny.cc/G1L2R4
- Lesson Ideas: Community Helpers: http://tiny.cc/G1L2R5
- Community Helpers Craft Idea: http://tiny.cc/G1L2R6

Grade 1 Lesson 3

"Inequality "

Time Frame: 60 minutes | **Subjects:** Math, Science |
Designer: Kara Howard
Standards: Zero Hunger (SDG 2), Achieve Gender Equality and Empower All Women and Girls (SDG 5), Reduce Inequality Within and Among Countries (SDG 10)

Summary and Rationale: This lesson will allow students to actively engage with the issue of inequality and will place this issue within the larger framework of building moral, empathetic, and ethical individuals.

Instructional Goal, Students will:
- Recognize and appreciate the interdependence of all people
- Learn how to be a good person
- Be aware of the scarcity of water, energy, and food
- Gain awareness of actions and responsibilities in an interconnected context
- Connect ethical values to content knowledge

Understanding Goal: Students will understand what inequality is and what it feels like to be affected by inequality. Students will begin to question why inequality happens and whether it is justified.

Essential Questions:
- What is inequality?
- How does inequality make us feel?
- How do we see it in our communities?
- Why does inequality happen?

Student Learning Objectives, Students will be able to:
- Identify examples of inequality
- Discussion emotions they connect to inequality
- Hypothesize why inequality happens

Assessment: Teachers can utilize informal checks for understanding during the activity, then formalize the assessment in a final collage of feelings they associate with inequality.

Sequence of Activities:

- **Introduction:** Teacher will introduce the topic of inequality as a concept of some people having something, when others do not. Teacher will relate inequality to the math concept of unequal ratios using the < sign. Using examples of 4<6 2<4 etc. Teacher will then use these examples to talk about how unequal amounts of things can be seen in our daily lives.

- **Activities:** Teacher will tell the class that she/he has brought some sweets to the class today. (Teacher can bring any type of sweet or snack that is contextually applicable and can be distributed in small pieces, ie M&Ms, toffees, pretzels, goldfish, etc.) The teacher will explain that the class is going to see how we can have moments in our lives that are unequal and that we going to do an activity that lets us talk about how we feel when this happens.

*Make sure to tell the students they should not eat the snacks until the very end of the lesson.

- **Teacher will:**
  - Distribute the majority of the snacks to one person, and one snack to every other child in the room.
  - Prompt the children to describe this distribution of snacks - whether it is equal or unequal.
  - Ask a few students who have one snack to talk about how they feel, when they only get one snack vs. the student who gets many.
  - Ask the student with many snacks to talk about how he feels in this situation.
  - Collect all the snacks and then redistribute them. This time the teacher will give an equal number of snacks to each of the boys in the class, but no snacks to the girls.
  - Elicit responses from individuals on both sides discussing their feelings about this distribution of snacks. The teacher will prompt with questions like: is it ok for boys to get more snacks than girls? Why not?

- ○ Collect all the snacks a final time. This redistribution will have 2 student with many snacks, a few more students (between 5-10 depending on class size) with 4-5 snacks, and then the rest of the students (the majority) with only 1 snack.
- ○ The teacher will again ask the students their perspectives on the distribution of snacks. Teacher will prompt with questions, "is this fair?"

- **Conclusion:** Teacher will then lead a discussion that asks students to pretend that what they had was not snacks, but instead water, or food. The teacher will prompt students to think about what it would mean if the students with the most snacks got to eat 3 meals a day, where the people with one snack only ate 1. Students will brainstorm about how they would feel in that situation. Students will brainstorm other things they see in the world that are distributed unequally - water, food, money, toys, clothes, etc. Finally the students will discuss what distribution would be best for everyone.

Resources for teachers:
- Mathematics and Social Justice in Grade 1: http://tiny.cc/G1L3R1

Grade 1 Lesson 4

"Equality and Fairness"

Time Frame: 50 minutes | **Subjects:** Civic education, Social Studies |
Designer: Nicolás Buchbinder
Standards: No Poverty (SDG 1), Zero Hunger (SDG 2), Decent Work and
Economic Growth (SDG 8), Reduced Inequalities (SDG 10), Peace, Justice,
and Strong Institutions (SDG 16)

Summary and rationale: This lesson will allow students to begin their
reflections on equality and fairness. Building on lesson 3, students will be
encouraged to think about material equality and whether specific contextual
situations require different distributions.

Instructional Goal, Students will:
- Understand the rights of all humans to lead happy, healthy, and
  productive lives regardless of gender, age, disability, etc. (no poverty,
  no hunger, etc);
- Understand the belief of basic equality of all people and their
  potential

Understanding: 1st grade students will initiate their understanding on equality
and fairness, experiencing and identifying moments and circumstances in
which everyone should receive the same and in which each person should
receive an individualized treatment.

Essential questions: How does inequality feel? What are the things that
every kid should have? Should we always be treated the same way?

Student Learning Objectives, Students Will be Able To:
- Propose and identify material elements that every kid should have;
- Interpret the problem presented in a children's literature piece or
  video;
- Understand that fair treatment can depend on circumstances.

Assessment: The teacher should encourage participation of all students to
make sure everybody is engaged in thinking about this topics.

Sequence of Activities:

- **Opener (5 minutes):** Recalling what happened in the last class. Teacher will ask students to remember what they did last class: What happened with the M&Ms and how did that activity make them feel in different moments of the class.

- **Activity #1 (15 minutes): Reflecting on equality**
  The teacher will ask students which would be the best way to distribute the M&Ms, directing students towards reflecting on equal distribution. After that, the teacher will ask the students what things they think every kid should have, and consider whether every children has access to those things.

- **Activity #2 (20 minutes): Fairness is not always giving the same to everyone**
  Teacher reads *"The fairest teacher of them all"* (http://tiny.cc/G1L4R1) by Jason Buckley.

  The teacher will ask students different questions about the reading: what happened in the story? why did Albert change his job? Was Albert doing the right things treating everyone the same? What should have Albert done?

- **Activity #3 (10 minutes): Sharing**
  In the last 10 minutes, some students will share what they did and the teacher will close with a commentary and reflection on equality and fairness.

Resources for teachers:

- (Reading) Fairest Teacher of Them All: http://tiny.cc/G1L4R1
- Teacher's Guide: http://tiny.cc/G1L4R2

Grade 1 Lesson 5

"Our very own declaration of human rights"

Time Frame: 60+ minutes | **Subjects:** ELA, Social Studies |
Designer: Chloé Suberville
Standards: Reduced Inequalities (SDG 10), Peace, Justice and Strong
Institutions (SDG 16)

Summary and Rationale: This lesson allows students to take action on skills
they learned, and to apply their knowledge of equality and inequality. As a
community they will use teamwork and communication to build a declaration
of human rights as part of their classroom community.

Instruction Goal: Students work together to apply their knowledge of
equality and inequality, and what it means to be a part of a larger community.

Understanding: Students will understand the meaning of creating a
document where we all agree on things that human beings deserve. Students
will work together to create a common document, for the greater good of the
community (classroom) where they understand the importance of such a
document.

Essential questions:
- What is a declaration of human rights?
- Why is it important to work together?
- How can we work together?
- How will we agree on what goes in this document?
- How do we represent all human rights we agree on?

Student Learning Objectives, Students will be able to:
- Work in teams to achieve a common goal
- Acquire tools for self-expression
- Apply their knowledge on equality and inequality
- Connect ethical values to content knowledge

Assessment: Teacher walks around during creation of classroom declaration of human rights, making sure students are working together. The final assessment will be the final declaration of human rights.

Sequence of Activities:

- **Opening: (10 minutes):**
  - ○ Teacher will ask students what they remember about being part of a community.
  - ○ What does it mean to be equal? Unequal?
  - ○ What are ways that we can all be happy members of a community?

- UDHR (10 minutes) Teacher will present some articles of the UDHR, (SIMPLIFIED VERSION) to students and discuss how this was created, explaining that a lot of people got together to create a document where all people would be treated nicely, and where people were would all be happy in the planet.

- **Democracy (5 minutes):**
  - ○ Teacher explains that they will come up with things that they want to be true in their classrooms, based on what they learned in the previous lessons, and they will make a document all together.
  - ○ Teacher explains that students will VOTE, so when they agree they should raise their hands and if the majority of the class agrees they can include it.

- **Creating articles (10 minutes):**
  - ○ Students come up with 10 articles for their declaration of human rights. If the majority of the class agrees they can include it.
  - ○ Students should be prompted to think about how fair the articles they are coming up with are, and how to make sure all students are included in their ideas.

- **Created UDHR: (10 minutes):**
  - ○ Students will be grouped into groups of 2-3, and will draw out, and write out words for each of the articles they have created. Each group will be focused on one of the articles, and will represent it using words and pictures.

○ Teacher will then bind all pictures and create one document for the classroom declaration of human rights.
○ Wrap up

Resources for Teachers:
- Universal Declaration of Human Rights (For Children): http://tiny.cc/G1L5R1

Grade 2

Lesson Overview
Learning Goal
Moving from the global to the local, learners will identify features of the global communities, their local community, their classmates, and finally themselves.
Lesson Scaffold

Lesson 1	Questioning the World Around Us
Lesson 2	Interviewing a Classmate
Lesson 3	Presenting Your Classmate
Lesson 4	Friendly Bar Graphs!
Lesson 5	Debriefing and Reflecting

Learning Objectives
• Students will explore and discover the diversity that exists in the classroom and the world. • Students will learn more about what makes other students in the class special. Students will become more curious and interested in other cultures. • Students will practice raising questions and performing active listening.

Grade 2 Lesson 1

**"Questioning the World Around Us:
Asking Questions About Culture, Place and Experience"**

Timeframe: 30 minutes | **Subjects:** Reading/Language Arts |
Designers: Ben Searle and Josie Papazis
Standards: Peace, Justice, and Strong Institutions (SDG 16)

Summary and Rationale: In this lesson, teachers will use a mentor text and photographs to incite interest and scaffold student inquiry. Students will then practice generating appropriate questions to ask others to learn about their culture, experiences, and background. By using visual supports, students are able to identify points of curiosity and will use teacher support to formulate appropriate and probing questions. Questioning is an essential component of building cultural understanding as well as a means to train students to be more metacognitive about their understanding of the world around them.

Learning Goal: In second grade, students will learn to:
- Understand the meaning of diversity
- Recognize the role diversity plays in day-to-day life.
- Identify and celebrate the value of diversity.

Understanding Goals: Students will learn how to structure thoughtful questions, and about the importance of learning from other's perspectives and experiences.

Essential Question:
- How are other people similar to use? How are they different from us?
- In what ways do people's experiences shape their opinions?
- What can we learn from other people that we cannot learn from other places?

Student Learning Objective: Students will be able to generate appropriate, inquiry-based questions about interests, home life and cultural practices using visual supports and modeled questioning.

Assessment: Student responses in reading discussion and group generated questions about the photo

Sequence of Activities:
- Teacher reads book, *Where Children Sleep* (http://tiny.cc/G2L1R1). Teacher chooses 3-4 children from the book and asks students what sort of questions they would ask some of the children in the book if they would like to know them better.
- Teacher should guide students towards more open ended questions that would generate more substantial responses.
- Teacher writes model questions on the board
- Teacher then posts 4 pictures of people from different cultural backgrounds, age/ethnic groups, to the class; ask students if they know anything/want to know anything about the people in the picture.
- In groups of three or four students generate five questions about one of the people in the photographs.

Resources for Teachers
- Where Children Sleep by James Molleson: http://tiny.cc/G2L1R1

Grade 2 Lesson 2

"Interviewing a Classmate"

Timeframe: 45 minutes | **Subjects:** English/Language Arts |
Designers: Josie Papazis, Ben Searle, Vijayaragavan Prabakaran
Standards: Peace, Justice and Strong Institutions (SDG 16), Partnership for
the Goals (SDG 17)

Summary and Rationale: Building off skills learned in Lesson 1, students
will build empathy and increase understanding of their peers though the
process of asking open ended questions and listening actively. Students will
track their classmates' responses to present in the next lesson.

Instructional Goal: Students will conduct peer interviews, taking notes for
later presentation.

Understanding: Students will understand that when they ask thoughtful,
open-ended questions and listen carefully, they can learn things from their
peers that they would have never known otherwise.

Essential Question:
- What do I already know about this person?
- What do I want to know about this person?
- Did anything I learned about this person surprise me? Did anything
  help me understand them better?
- What do I want to know now? How can I best ask questions to find
  out that information?

Student Learning Objectives, Students Will be Able To :
- Generate open-ended questions through writing.
- Identify the interests and backgrounds of another student through
  active listening

Assessment: Student presentations

Sequence of Activities:

- **Part 1:**

Teacher leads instruction on identifying and generating open ended questions
Open-ended questions can help us discover what makes other people <u>unique</u>
<u>and special</u>.

There is no right or wrong answer to an open ended question.
An open-ended can't be answered with "Yes" or "No"

- **Part 2:**

  Each student copies down the 4 example open-ended questions
  above. Then each student creates one or two new open-ended
  questions of their own. (Ex. "Tell me..?", "What... ?", "How...?", or
  "Why...?").

- **Part 3:** Working in pairs, students will use their list of questions to
  interview their partner to learn more about them. Students should
  take turns asking questions and listening carefully.

  Student challenge: Students should document what they learn about
  their partner by writing down key words or draw pictures to help
  them remember what they learn about your partner.

  Sample questions for students to use:
  - ○ *Tell me about your happiest memory?*
  - ○ *What does it mean to be a "good friend"?*
  - ○ *How do you get to school in the morning?*
  - ○ *Why do you like school?*

- **Part 4:** Teacher will lead a whole group reflection discussion using
  these guiding questions:
  - ○ *Can someone share with the class one new thing they learned about their partner?*
  - ○ *Did you discover anything that you and your partner have in common?*
  - ○ *How are you and your partner different?*
  - ○ *How did you feel, when your partner asked you an open-ended question?*
  - ○ *If everybody was the same, would that be good? What do you think?*

Grade 2 Lesson 3

"Presenting Your Classmate"

Timeframe: 30 minutes | **Subject:** Language Arts |
Designers: Josie Papazis, Ben Searle, Vijayaragavan Prabakaran
Standards: Peace, Justice and Strong Institutions (SDG 16), Partnership for the Goals (SDG 17)

Summary and Rationale: In this lesson, students will present the findings of their interviews with their peers. To scaffold accordingly teachers will present guiding questions to support student presentations. By sharing their findings, students will build classroom community and support intercultural understanding.

Instructional Goal: Students will present findings of their peer interviews with the class.

Understanding: When we all ask thoughtful questions and listen carefully, we can find out things about our class we would have never known otherwise and build more meaningful friendships.

Essential Question:
- What did I learn from my interview? How do I want to present it to the class?
- What did I learn from other people's interviews?
- How does this new information impact our class community and my relationships with my classmates?

Student Learning Objectives, Students Will be Able To:
- Actively recall their interview from the last session
- Present three to five new things they learned about their classmates.

Sequence of Activities:

- **Part 1:** Building off the previous activity, each student will stand up and share a few positive things about their partner that they learned. Students will use the following questions as a guide:

71

- ○ *Who are they?*
- ○ *What are they like?*
- ○ *Why are they special?*
- ○ *How are they different from you?*
- ○ *What do you like about interviewing your partner?*
- ○ *Were you uncomfortable asking questions? Why do you think so?*

- **Part 2:** As an extension: students can create a poem, a dance, a drawing, or bring a small gift to present to their partner that celebrates or illustrates something they like about their partner.

- **Part 3:** Teacher will lead students in a reflection after all presentations are done using the following guiding questions:
  - ○ *Can someone share how they felt when their partner said something nice about them?*
  - ○ *Can someone share how they felt when they said something nice about their partner?*
  - ○ *Why does it feel good to say nice things?*
  - ○ *Why do you think it is good to be different or unique?*

Grade 2 Lesson 4

"Friendly Bar Graphs"

Time: 40 minutes | **Subjects:** Language Arts/Math |
Designer: Vijayaragavan Prabakaran
Standards: Peace, Justice and Strong Institutions (SDG 16), Partnership for the Goals (SDG 17), Good Health and Well-Being (SDG 3)

Summary and Rationale: Teacher will model how to collect and represent data in bar graphs in order for students to quantify different perspectives in their class and understand commonalities within their classroom communities.

Instructional Goal: Students will learn about different ways to present information from teacher modeling.

Understanding: The way I present information is just as important as the actual information itself, and I must think carefully about what I want my audience to learn from my presentations.

Essential Question:
- How do we most commonly present information?
- What types of presentation are best for different types of information? Numerical data? Interviews?
- How does the way in which I present information affect how people view that information?

Sequence of Activities:

Teacher facilitates student discussion about the qualities of a good friend and organize data into a simple bar graphs.

Suggested script:

"What is one word you would use to describe a friend? What makes a good friend? Think about a friend or a person you like to spend time with, and write down two or three words that describe him or her."

73

Optional: The teacher may choose to write a list of adjectives on the board for kids to choose from.

"Now, as each of you tell me a word that describes a good friend, I am going to write that down."

<Writes on the board>

"Oh, there's so many great words on the board, and some of you said the same words. Wouldn't it be cool if we had a way of showing the most common qualities of a good friend in a graph?"

<Teacher categorizes data, models counting of each category and writes the number>

Nice - 5, Funny - 7, Helpful - 3, Smart - 4, Honest - 1

"Fantastic! Now, we are going to learn how to show this in a picture with bars."

<Teacher draws the bar graph - tells the students that the categories are on the bottom line and the number will be the vertical line, draws the bars from the data>

This is very interesting! Now we can know the most important qualities of a good friend just by looking at this picture. This is also called a bar graph.

<Teacher checks for understanding?

"Now, we are going to do another bar graph but together. <Teacher cold calls or picks a student who asks a question he is interested to know about for the whole class - Example - what is your favorite color/bird/animal/food."

<Teacher facilitates the student to collect data and write it in number (abstract) form, and then to draw it as a bar graph>

Options for Independent Practice:
Student teams use the data they already have collected from the previous lessons about their friends - and represent that data in graphs.
Student teams do a project outside the class - on questions that would lay the foundation for SDG competencies.

- How many times were you kind this week?
- How many of your friends speak a different language?
- How many times did you share food?

Grade 2 Lesson 5

"Debriefing and Reflecting"

Timeframe: 20 minutes | **Subjects:** Language Arts/Math |
Designers: Ben Searle and Josie Papazis
Standards: Peace, Justice and Strong Institutions (SDG 16), Partnership for the Goals (SDG 17)

Summary and Rationale: It is important to ensure students are meta-cognitive about the importance of questioning and why we use questions to build bridges. Through guided reflection, students will reflect on the importance of the process and discuss how to transfer the skills to contexts outside the classroom in order to ask questions of their peers and the world around them.

Instructional Goal: Students will consider what they have learned about thoughtful questioning, and reflect on how they can bring these take-aways into their everyday life.

Understanding: The skills I have learned from interviewing my classmates are also applicable to my relationships with other people outside of class, and I should continue to ask thoughtful questions and listen actively in my life.

Essential Question:
- What did I learn about posing questions and interpreting answers from this project?
- Was there anything that surprised me, or I had never before considered?
- Are there any other settings in which these skills might be valuable? If so, what are they?

Student Learning Objectives, Students Will be Able To:
- Reflect on the interview and inquiry process
- Share their reflections with the class

Sequence of Activities:
- **Teachers will lead the class in the following Questions**
  - What was difficult about this process?

77

- o Was it easy talking with your partner?
- o What did you learn about your partner that you didn't know before?

- **Some target themes and responses:**
  - o Accepting differences/tolerating
  - o Collaborative learning
  - o Classmates who are so different from you are in the same classroom, just as smart, etc.

Grade 3

Lesson Overview	
Learning Goal	
Students will understand the origins and the complex systems which are required to produce food and how these systems intimately impact the lives of humans around the world. Students will forge an ethical orientation towards our natural resources and all other forms of life - on land and water - and understand our common responsibility to preserve/conserve our planet for sustainability.	
Lesson Scaffold	
Lesson 1	**Origins of Food**
Lesson 2	**Farming Cultures with Guest Speaker**
Lesson 3	**How Plants Grow**
Lesson 4	**Class Garden**
Lesson 5	**Food In Complex Systems**
Learning Objectives	
<ul><li>Students will learn about a new topic and share knowledge with their peers.</li><li>Students will think critically about how an issue affects their own lives.</li><li>Students will participate in a hands-on project, working with the peers to produce a final product.</li></ul>	

Grade 3 Lesson 1
"Origins of Food"

Time Frame: 60 minutes | **Subjects:** Science, Social Studies, Health
Standards, SDGs: No Poverty (SDG 1), Zero Hunger (SDG 2), Good
Health and Well-Being (SDG 3), Responsible Production and Consumption
(SDG 12).

Summary and Rationale: Students will use their own lunch to discuss the
origins of their food, where it comes from, and relate their meals to issues of
poverty and hunger worldwide.

Instructional Goal: Students will develop an appreciation of food
differences globally and understand the equality issues related to food
distribution in different contexts.

Understanding Goals:

- The delivery of food from the farm to the table involves complex
  technologies and delivery chains
- People in other cultures eat different foods because of geographic
  characteristics as well as issues of access
- Access (or lack of access) to different foods is related to inequalities
  such as health and poverty

Essential questions:

- Where does our food come from?
- Why do different cultures consume different foods?
- How is food access unequally distributed throughout the world?

Student Learning Objectives, Students Will be Able To:

- Identify the origins of food production
- Compare and contrast differences in food cultures
- Discuss injustices related to food access and nutrition across the
  world

Assessment:
- 1-2 sentence answers to final questions at the end of the lesson
- Maps of food production created by students

Sequence of Activities:

- **Hook (10 minutes):** *What's for lunch today?*
  - Describe and draw a picture of what you brought/what the school offers for lunch. What types of foods are you eating? Where did these foods come from? (the ground? an animal?)
  - *Discuss: Where did your food come from today? What had to happen in order from the food to get from where it started (the farm) to your plate?*
  - Teacher should have students draw a healthy plate divided into four groups (fruit, vegetables, protein, grain). This will help them analyze inequalities in food consumption in the next activity

- **Activity #1 (20 minutes):** *Picture analysis*
  - Give students pictures (or written cards with food names, or drawings, if unable to print) of ten lunches from different countries around the world, including countries of different income status. Some of the lunches should be lacking in protein or fruit, for example, or plates with barely any food, while others should be overflowing or abundant.
  - **Step 1:** *Partner Work (5 minutes):* In partners, students will use their healthy plate to identify which school lunches are well-rounded and which components of a healthy meal are missing. Students will sort and rank the pictures of meals based on quality. (5 minutes)
  - **Step 2:** *Group Work (3 minutes):* In groups of four, students will compare how and why they sorted the meals the way they did. Students will note differences and common choices and share their thinking. (3 minutes)
  - **Step 3:** *Whole Class (12 minutes):* Students share which countries they found had well-rounded meals and which were lacking.

  - **Discussion Questions:**
    - What can you guess about these countries' farms?

- What type of food do these countries seem to have access to?
- Why do you think some places have more food than others?
- How do you feel when you are hungry? Are you able to focus?
- How do you think being hungry might affect your focus in school?

- **Activity #2 (20 minutes): Food Production Map**
  - Students are introduced to the delivery chain of food by drawing a map (see example at end of lesson) in small groups on poster paper. The teacher should ask students what steps they imagine must happen for them to have lunch today. As a class, create an outline for the map and have students draw and label the process in groups.

- **Conclusion/Assessment:** Students write answers to the following questions.
  1. How does food get from the farm to your table?
  2. Why are some lunches unequal in different places?

Resources for students:
- Pictures of school lunches in different countries: http://tiny.cc/G3L1R1
- A healthy plate: http://tiny.cc/G3L1R2
- Diagram of farm to table process : http://tiny.cc/G3L1R3

Resources for teachers:
- Why teaching food origins is important : http://tiny.cc/G3L1R4

Grade 3 Lesson 2

"Farming Culture and Guest Speaker"

Time Frame: 60 minutes | **Subjects:** Science and Social Studies |
Designer: Chihiro Yoshida
Standards: No Poverty (SDG 1), No Hunger (SDG 2), Good Health and
Well Being (SDG 3), Decent Work and Economic Growth (SDG 8),
Sustainable Cities and Communities (SDG 11), Climate Action (SDG 13), Life
on Land (SDG 15)

Summary and Rationale: Students will be taught about various farming
cultures around the world, be exposed to and engage in a conversation with
an adult who is in the occupation of farming from a nearby community.

Instructional Goal:
- Students will gain an understanding of various forms of agriculture
  around the world.
- Students will gain a better understanding of occupations in
  agriculture.

Understanding Goals:
- There are various forms of agriculture and means of production
  around the world.
- Differences stem from cultural, societal, economic factors.
- There are individuals within your own community who work in
  agriculture.

Essential questions:
- What are the different types of agricultural products around the
  world?
- How are foods produced around the world?
- What role does agriculture play in society in different cultures?
- What are the raw experiences of people in your own community that
  work in agriculture?

Student Learning Objectives, Students Will be Able To:
- Compare and contrast differences in agricultural production around the world
- Identify the roles that people in agricultural occupations play within the community
- Relate to and emphasize with current issues faced by people working in agriculture within their own community

Assessment: Individual reflections and/or letters written to Guest Speaker

Sequence of Activities:

- **Opener (5 minutes):**
  Discussion: Who knows people who work in agriculture? What do they do? How are they involved in the food producing process? What is their role in society?

- **Introduction (15 minutes):**
  Presentation: The classroom teacher will introduce various people around the world who are involved in agriculture and their local processes and issues (US - cornfields, machinery; Japan - rice paddies, smaller family-based manufacturing; India - sugar canes, farmer suicides).

- **Core event (30 minutes):**
  Guest Speaker: Someone who works in agricultural production will be invited to speak to the classroom. Ideally, it would be someone who is involved in agriculture with an entrepreneurial mindset and a vision of changing the way that agricultural business is operated.

  Q&A: The classroom teacher will facilitate questions and follow-up discussion between the guest speaker and students.

- **Reflection (10 minutes):**
  Concluding remarks and individual reflection (journal writing and/or letter writing to Guest Speaker)

Resources for students:
- The Man Who Fed the World: http://tiny.cc/G3L2R1
- The Kid Who Changed the World (children's book): http://tiny.cc/G3L2R2

- The Day the Crayons Quit (children's book) - http://tiny.cc/G3L2R3

Resources for teachers:
- Norman Borlaug - World Food Prize: http://tiny.cc/G3L2R4
- Norman Borlaug - Genius Behind the green Revolution: http://tiny.cc/G3L2R5
- Urban Farming Around the World: http://tiny.cc/G3L2R6
- Agriculture's Importance within the Economy: http://tiny.cc/G3L2R7
- Green Bronx Machine: http://tiny.cc/G3L2R8
- Entrepreneurship in Agriculture - http://tiny.cc/G3L2R10
- America's Farmers: http://tiny.cc/G3L2R14

Grade 3 Lesson 3

"How Plants Grow"

Time Frame: 60 minutes | **Subjects**: Biology, Food Sciences | **Designer:** Matt Owens

Standards: Clean Water and Sanitation (SDG 6); Responsible Consumption and Production (SDG 12); Climate Action (SDG 13); Life on Land (SDG 15)

Summary and Rationale: Students will explore the life cycle of plants in order to understand how plants grow and produce food as well as how humans are able to influence and alter this process.

Instructional Goal:
- Students will learn what resources plants needs to thrive and produce food suitable for humans.
- The students will utilize this knowledge to plan a classroom garden that will be implemented in the following lesson.

Understanding Goals:
- Plants need clean water and air, good soil, sunlight, and care to grow and produce food
- The food we eat is interconnected to complex ecosystems that humans have the ability to impact in positive or negative ways

Essential Questions:
- How do plants produce the food we eat? What do they need to grow?
- How do we help plants grow?

Student Learning Objectives, Students Will be Able To:
- Identify the steps of the plant life-cycle and the different resources a plant needs to thrive (clean air and water, good soil, sunlight, care)
- Identify simple steps they can take to care for plants
- Utilize this knowledge to plan a classroom garden that will be implemented in the following lesson.

Assessment:
- Informal checks for comprehension as students plan the garden;

- Life cycle diagram;
- Garden plan

Sequence of Activities:

- ***Hook: Reflect and Discuss (10 minutes)***
  The teacher leads the class in a reflection on the farmer's visit in the previous lesson. The teacher prompts students with questions about the different types of food the farmer grows, how he grows the food, leading into a discussion of what food needs to grow and how humans might be able to help.

- ***Discover: The Plant Life Cycle (20 minutes)***
  Teacher transitions the lesson to an exploration of the plant life cycle. Suggested mediums to introduce the topic include children's books and video clips that show the life cycle of a plant and how people can help plants grow. The teacher then leads the class in a discussion of the different parts of the plant and its different stages, focusing on the things a plant needs to grow strong and healthy.

  Optional Activity: in order to assess student understanding, students draw diagrams of the plant life cycle in order to demonstrate how plants grow and produce food, and what they need to do so.

- ***Connect: Design a Class Garden (20 minutes)***
  Students draw and design their own garden, including a plan of what they can do to make sure the plant grows. Students are then invited to share their plan with partners or in small groups.

- ***Plan: Looking Forward (10 minutes)***
  The teacher then brings the class back together to discuss and explain to students the plan for the next lesson: building a class garden.

Resources for students:
- *Video Clips*
  - How Does It Grow: http://tiny.cc/G3L3R1
  - How Food Grows: http://tiny.cc/G3L3R2
  - From Seed To Flower: http://tiny.cc/G3L3R3

- *Children's Books*

- o Eddie's Garden And How to Make Things Grow: http://tiny.cc/G3L3R4
- o First Peas to the Table: http://tiny.cc/G3L3R5
- o The Carrot Seed: http://tiny.cc/G3L3R6

- *Online Exploration*
  - o The Great Plant Escape: http://tiny.cc/G3L3R7
  - o Parts of a Plant: http://tiny.cc/G3L3R8

Resources for teachers:

- *Garden Plans and Guides*
  - o Creating School Gardens: http://tiny.cc/G3L3R9
  - o Gardens for Learning: http://tiny.cc/G3L3R10

- *Other Resources*
  - o Plant Parts: http://tiny.cc/G3L3R11
  - o Agriculture Literacy Curriculum: http://tiny.cc/G3L3R12

Grade 3 Lesson 4

"Class Garden"

Time Frame: 60+ minutes | **Subjects:** Social Studies/Life-Skills | **Designer:** Cassie Fuenmayor

Standards: No Poverty (SDG 1), No Hunger (SDG 2), Good Health and Well Being (SDG 3), Decent Work and Economic Growth (SDG 8), Sustainable Cities and Communities (SDG 11), Climate Action (SDG 13), Life on Land (SDG 15)

Summary and Rationale: This lesson will center around implementation of the class garden designed in lesson 3. It will promote creativity, agency and action, as well as self-reliance and community development.

Instructional Goals:

- Students will cultivate an appreciation, curiosity, and respect for cultural diversity
- Students will practice teamwork and community development
- Students will use their own agency to implement a hands on project

Competencies:

- Cultivate an appreciation, curiosity, and respect for cultural diversity and world culture as the foundation for self-reflection, identity formation, and empathetically approaching human interaction, forms of life - on land and water - and understand our responsibility to preserve/conserve our planet for sustainability.
- Understand the elements of trust and collaboration, decent and gainful employment and why it is important to making and sustaining relationships both locally and globally.
- Acquire skills in economics and financial relations, science, technology, data analysis, and health that will allow students to address real world issues.
- Analyze and researching solutions to problems (water, energy, and food) from the perspectives of different roles, such as consumers,

93

businesses, scientists, policy makers, researchers, retailers, media, and development cooperation agencies, among others.

Understanding Goal: Students will understand the importance of teamwork and collaboration as well as agency and action in the implementation of a project plan.

Essential questions:
- Who will do what task when implementing the garden, what strategies will they use to complete their task?
- What do we need to do to keep our garden healthy? Who will take responsibility for these tasks?
- How does our garden compare to what we've learned about agriculture? How is it similar/different?
- How can we share our garden with our school/community?

Student Learning Objectives, Students Will be Able To:
- Implement the garden design planned in Lesson 3
- Complete his/her assigned task in the garden creation
- Exercise their own agency in deciding the best way to complete their assigned tasks
- Engage with each other to help complete their tasks

Assessment: To assess this lesson, teachers can compare the completed garden with the plan/design for the garden.

Sequence of Activities:

- **5-10 Min - Hook:** Review garden design and assigned tasks. Students spend 5-10 minutes planning how they will complete their task.
- **50 Min - Main:** Students will complete their assigned task according to garden plan with the help of each other and the teacher.
- **5 Min - Conclusion:** students will clean up and spend 5 minutes discussing with peers if they think the garden went according to plan. What went well? What challenges did they face? How did they meet these challenges?

Resources for teachers:
- Growing Minds - School Gardens: http://tiny.cc/G3L4R1

Grade 3 Lesson 5

"Food in Complex Systems: Harkness Discussion "

Time Frame: 60 minutes | **Subjects**: Social Studies, Biology, Food Sciences, Health, Economics
Designer: Christian Bautista

Standards: No Poverty (SDG 1), Zero Hunger (SDG 2), Good Health and Well-Being (SDG 3), Clean Water and Sanitation (SDG 6), Decent Work and Economic Growth (SDG 8), Industry Innovation and Infrastructure (SDG 9), Reduced Inequalities (SDG 10), Sustainable Cities and Communities (SDG 11), Responsible Consumption and Growth (SDG 12), Life on Land (SDG 15), Partnerships for the Goals (SDG 17)

Summary and Rationale: After students have imagined, planned, and executed their Class Garden project, the class will reflect upon their activity and connect it with local and global issues such as poverty, hunger, sharing, markets, and justice.

Instructional Goal: Students will be able to identify, consider, and address the secondary effects of food growth, markets, famine, and poverty.

Understanding Goals: Food growth and consumption is deeply connected to complex systems that intimately affect individual human lives around the world. The interplay of these various systems have implications for human rights, sustainability, and global equity.

Essential questions:
- After building our class garden, how much harder would it be to design a farm that fed the entire school? An entire city?
- If we built this farm, what would happen if we weren't able to grow any food?
- What if we didn't have enough money to build our garden or to maintain it?
- If the 4th grade class built a different type of garden and ours grew food but theirs didn't, what could we do to help them?

- What are some ways that, ahead of time, we could make sure that we would all have enough food?

Student Learning Objectives

Students Will be Able To:
- Draw upon their experiences over the last 4 lessons to contribute to a deep discussion on issues adjacent to food production and consumption.
- Engage in a Harkness discussion, where the teacher will pose challenging, open ended questions as suggested in the Lesson 5 Essential Questions above; students will answer these questions and respond to one another's answers in a discussion rather than a debate format.
- Contribute to the discussion - teachers should ensure that 100% of students add to the discussion and that it is not dominated by particular students - if the students have not previously been exposed to Socratic or Harkness discussions, time should be spent going over expectations and norms.
- Keep a positive attitude towards one another's contributions and will connect their learning to larger, global issues.

Assessment:
- The lesson will include both informal, organic assessment by the teacher (noting interesting contributions by specific students) as well as two formal assessments by the teacher. If she chooses, the teacher may "grade" the class as a group by using a rubric to assess the quality of the discussion (did all students speak? did the class stay on topic? were attitudes positive rather than combative?). The teacher will also have students reflect briefly upon one or to essential questions in writing; these reflections can be assessed afterwards by the teacher.

Sequence of Activities:

Introduction (5 minutes)
- The teacher will explain to students that class time today will be devoted to reflecting on all that they have learned so far. The teacher will also direct students to arrange their desks/seats in a circle, with the teacher included in that circle.

Discussion (30 minutes)

- The teacher will lead a discussion of the 5 essential questions outlined above. Students should engage with each other's thoughts, with the teacher only prompting further discussion or challenging statements.

Debrief/Wrap up (10 minutes)
- The teacher will spend a few minutes talking to the class about today's discussion, and allowing students to share how they felt or what they learned. Prior to leaving class, each student should write down one thing that they learned from the discussion that they had not known or considered previously.

Grade 4

Lesson Overview
Learning Goal
This unit helps students develop a sense of their position in relations to the wider world, and understanding how elements in the world relate to each other in reference to one's own values. The unit is designed to be a sequence of five lessons, though each lesson can be employed independently. Each lesson is also designed to preempt the concepts introduced in the next lesson.
Lesson Scaffold

Lesson 1	Developing Self-Identities
Lesson 2	Learning About the Environment
Lesson 3	Nations and Resources
Lesson 4	SDGs and Actionable Steps
Lesson 5	Tying it All Together

Learning Objectives
<ul><li>Students will think about and describe their own identities, as well as their place within the wider world.</li><li>Students will identify ways they can contribute to the health of the environment and reduce waste.</li><li>Students will collaborate on a final project and practice performing in front of their peers.</li></ul>

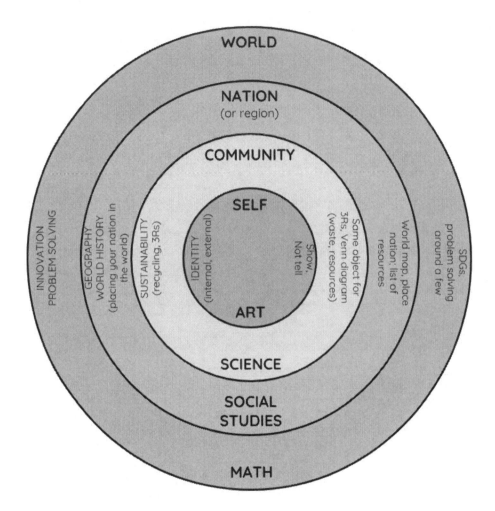

Grade 4 Lesson 1

"Self - Identity Development"

Time Frame: 45 minutes | **Subjects:** Arts (Fine Art and Language Arts) | **Designer:** Quinn Lockwood
Standards: Peace, Justice, and Strong Institutions (SDG 16)

Summary and Rationale: Students will start the series of five lessons that will help them develop global competencies. Students will be exploring notions of identity, starting with the question "Who am I?" Learning will include a discussion of individual identities as well as those of their classmates (internal identity, such as interests and values, as well as external identity, such as appearance and dress). This should include some discussion that prompts students to think about how values shape their identities. They will discuss what things are important to them, why those things matter, and start thinking about what their families and others they interact with may value, and imaging what people around the world may value.

Instructional Goal: Students will begin to explore the concept of identity. They will look specifically at the way that identities are shaped by a variety of factors, with a focus on values as a major force that determines identity. Students will be asked to talk about themselves, their interests, and what is important to them. They will also make connections between their own values and those of their classmates — including listing those that are shared and those that are not. Students should be able to discuss what might happen when people do not share values, and come up with strategies for getting along with others who may not value the same things. Students should be guided in beginning to understand why different people value different things.

Understanding: That many things shape our identities, that our values play an important role in determining who we are, and that different people may value different things.

Essential questions:
- What do we mean when we talk about "identity?"
- What are some different ways we can answer the question "Who am I?"

- What are some examples of things that form our identities?
- What are the things that are important to us?
- Why do we feel that these things are important?
- What are some things that our classmates, friends and neighbors feel are important?
- Do we think those things are important too?
- How can we get along with people who think other things are important?

Student Learning Objectives, Students Will be Able To:
- Feel comfortable talking about themselves and the things that make them "them."
- Talk about many different components of their identities, including the things that matter most to them.
- Look for similarities and differences between their values and those of their classmates.
- Represent themselves in pictures and words.
- Take turns in speaking and responding to their classmates.
- Understand that differences should be celebrated.

Assessment: Students' individual storybooks

Sequence of activities:

- **Introduce the topic (5 minutes)** Tell students that they are going to do an exercise to show ways that people are similar and different. Teacher can begin by marking a circle on the floor in the middle of the room. It will need to be large enough for all students to be able to fit inside at once. This may require some preparation of furniture in the room (moving desk to the side, etc.) Invite students to come into the circle if they can answer "yes" to certain questions: "Come into the circle if you wear glasses/have brown hair/have a sister/have been to another country/speak a different language/like to eat vegetables" etc. Finish by saying "Come into the circle if you are in Mr./Mrs. [teacher's name] class at [school]!" All children will finish together in the circle.

- **Answer the question "Who am I?" (10 minutes)** Students will brainstorm answers to the question, "Who am I?" based on some examples provided that complete the question "I am someone who…" For this part of the exercise, students can give more surface-level answers based on interests, hobbies and abilities like "I am someone who likes ice cream" or "I am someone who can run really fast." This can be done as a class on the board or individually on worksheets. Teacher can guide the students to notice the similarities and differences in their answers (for example, did several students say "I am someone who likes…" or "I am someone who can…"?) Teacher can also take this time to start prompting students to think about the ways that someone living in a different part of the world might answer these questions.

- **Introduce the idea of values (5 minutes)** Teacher will ask students to think more deeply about their identities, in terms of what matters to them and what things they think are important. As a class, they can add these things to their existing lists, and go through the same process of seeing what things they have in common. Students may need some examples of this before they can do it themselves, like "I am someone who thinks my family is important" or "I am someone who thinks it is important to be kind to others."

- **Introduce activity (2-3 minutes)** Teacher explains that students are going to create their own personal storybooks. Teacher shows his/her own book that answers specific prompts on each page by writing, drawing or both. Teacher passes out blank books to students along with a variety of art supplies.

- **Students begin their art/language art project (~25 minutes)** Students use remaining class time to work on their storybooks. Ideally, students will finish with enough time to show one another their individual stories and notice some things in the stories that are the same. The books could be turned into a classroom display.

Resources for teachers:
Learning Area 1: Who Am I? http://tiny.cc/G3L4R1
Individual and Community Identity - Lesson Plans: http://tiny.cc/G4L1R2

Grade 4 Lesson 2

"Community/Society - Ecology "

Time Frame: 45 mins | **Subjects:** Science | **Designer:** Sharon Jiae Lee
Standards: Clean Water and Sanitation (SDG 6), Affordable and Clean Energy (SDG 7), Reduced Inequalities (SDG 10), Sustainable Cities and Communities (SDG 11), Responsible Consumption and Production (SDG 12), Climate Action (SDG 13), Life Below Water (SDG 14), Life on Land (SDG 15)

Summary and Rationale: In lesson 1, students have learned what values are and have identified and shared about their individual values. In this lesson, students will broaden their definition of values by connecting their individual values to the values of the community, especially in regards to the issue of promoting a sustainable environment. They will learn about the Three Rs (Reduce, Reuse, Recycle) and come up with ways to turn waste in the community into resources. *NOTE: The teacher will bring one type of waste (e.g. paper, cans, bottles, plastic bags, etc.) that is most prominent in the context of the community. The waste chosen for this lesson plan is bottles but this can be adapted.

Instructional Goals (overarching goal): Students will be able to reflect and learn about how to create a sustainable community. They will accomplish the overarching goal by 1. (*Feel*) Showing awareness that wastes can be turned into resources; 2. (*Think*) Demonstrating knowledge in the Three Rs (Reduce, Reuse, Recycle); 3. (*Act*) Putting the awareness and knowledge into action by creating an innovative way to turn a waste in the community into a resource.

Understanding Goals:
- Wastes are harmful to the environment of our communities and the world.
- Wastes don't have to remain as wastes but can be turned into useful resources by using innovative ideas
- Creative thinking needs to be accompanied with action to cause positive change in our communities and the world.

Essential questions:

- What are the Three Rs? (Reduce, Reuse, Recycle)
- What wastes do we see around us in our community?
- How can we turn the wastes in our community into useful resources?

Student Learning Objectives (Students Will be Able To): with Assessment Checklist:

Objective	Conditions	Observable Skill/Behavior	Assessment
Define and explain what the Three Rs are	In small groups (teacher goes around making sure all groups understand the concept of the Three Rs	They will discuss in small groups	Can the students define what the Three Rs are? Can they give an example for each?
Presenting in class on wastes in their community	Working in groups or individually and presenting in front of class	Depending on the size of the classroom, students can either: 1. split into groups and come up with a list of observation of wastes in their community and have one representative per group present in front of class or 2. have each student present one waste in their community	Is the student participating in the discussion? Is the student working collaboratively to create a list of wastes? Is the student presenting in a manner that is clear to understand?
Coming up with a creative way to turn a waste that the teacher has brought into something reusable	In groups or individually	In groups or individually, students will turn the item that the teacher has brought into something reusable.	❏ Does the student have a finished product that has been turned from waste into something reusable?

Sequence of Activities:

- **Opening: 6 mins**

  Reviewing Lesson 1 -Ask students what they remember from Lesson 1. Students should be able to talk about their individual values.

  - **Questions:** *Who can remember what values are? Can anyone share their values? Can we still be friends if our values are different?*

    Introduce to the students that in this lesson, they will be learning about the values

    of their community.

  - **Questions:** *Can anyone tell me what you think is important for your family? What is one important value in our community?*

    After hearing some answers, narrow down the topic to the values of the

    community in regards to sustainable environment.

  - **Questions:** *What do you think our community thinks about the environment? About Nature? Do we respect nature? Why or why not?*

- **The Three Rs: 14 mins**

  - Introduce the concept and effects of waste: (Waste is anything that we throw away)

    - Show the effects of waste on the environment through pictures: simply throwing waste away causes pollution, water contamination, soil contamination

    - Emphasize the fact that simply throwing away waste is very harmful to the community

    - Divide students into groups and have them discuss about wastes that they see in their community OR have students brainstorm individually (depending on class size)

    - Have some representatives present the list of wastes that they came up with

    - **Questions:** *What is waste? What do you think are the effects of waste?*

    - What should we do? There is something that every one of us can do.

* Divide students into groups. For each of the Three R concepts, define the concept and have the students brainstorm ways to apply the concept.

○ Introduce the concept of The Three Rs:
  - Reduce: reducing is the best way to help the environment. Have students brainstorm ways to reduce everyday things in their small groups (e.g. Instead of buying something, you could borrow. Save water by using less when you brush your teeth.)
  - Reuse: instead of throwing things away, we can try to find ways to use them again. Brainstorm ways (e.g. Instead of using plastic bags, bring a cloth bag when going grocery shopping. Instead of using paper/plastic cups, carry your own mug).
  - Recycle: Most things that can't be reused CAN be recycled. Brainstorm ways you can do this (e.g. divide up different materials and throw them away separately)

○ **Questions:** *What should we do about waste in our community? What are the Three Rs? What does it mean to reduce? What does it mean to reuse? What does it mean to recycle?*

- **Activity: 15 mins**
  ○ In their groups (or individually), distribute a bottle to each student and ask them to turn the bottle into something creative that they can *reuse*.
  ○ Provide the students with scissors, tape, glue, color papers as needed
  ○ Have students collaborate with each other by bouncing off ideas from each other, respectfully listening to different ideas, and coming up with a creative solution to the problem.
  ○ After 10 minutes of activities, spend 5 minutes having each group (or individual) present what they did with their bottles.

  ○ **Questions:** *How can we turn this waste into something useful?*

- **Closing: 5 Min**
  Emphasize again the effects of waste on the environment. Ask the students what the Three Rs were to help the environment. And end the class by reminding them that there is something that each of us can do to help the environment.

○ **Questions:** *What have we learned about waste today? How do the Three R's help the environment? What could we do to help the environment?*

Resources for students:
- Waste Management: http://tiny.cc/G4L2R1
- Kids NIH: http://tiny.cc/G4L2R2
- Video Song for Three Rs: http://tiny.cc/G4L2R3

Resources for teachers:
- Definition of waste: http://tiny.cc/G4L2R4
- Waste effect on the environment: http://tiny.cc/G4L2R5
- Trash to Treasure: http://tiny.cc/G4L2R6
- Curriculum and Activities for Kids and Teachers: http://tiny.cc/G4L2R7
- The 3 Rs of the Environment: http://tiny.cc/G4L2R8
- (Video) Creative ways to recycle bottles: http://tiny.cc/G4L2R9

Grade 4 Lesson 3

"Nation - World History, Geography "

Time Frame: 45 minutes | **Subjects:** Social Studies |
Designer: Holing Yip
Standards: No Poverty (SDG 1), Zero Hunger (SDG 2), Clean Water and
Sanitation (SDG 6), Affordable and Clean Energy (SDG 7), Decent Work and
Economic Growth (SDG 8), Industry, Innovation, and Infrastructure (SDG
9), Responsible Consumption and Production (SDG 12), Partnership for the
Goals (SDG 17)

Summary and Rationale: Once the students have gained awareness of the
physical objects in their surrounding as waste and resources from the previous
lesson, in this lesson they will learn about how the exchange of resources (and
sometimes waste) connect different nations and regions. Through
investigating where their everyday resources are from, students will gain an
understanding that nations and regions are interrelated and interdependent. In
addition, in preparation for the next lesson on the world, students will get a
sense of how this interrelatedness affects global dynamics of interaction.

Instructional Goal: Students will be able to reason why certain objects can
be produced in their place of origin, and, if applicable, why these resources
have been imported. For students who have already been introduced the use
of mind maps, they will be able to record their ideas using mind maps, and
form arguments using the mind map as a guide. Students will be able to
articulate some pros and cons of regional and global interdependence.

Understanding Goal: That some of their daily resources are produced within
their nation or region, and some are produced in other places; that the regions
are interconnected through the exchange of resources.

Essential questions:
- Where is this object produced?
- How far is the place of origin from us?
- What circumstances and resources do we need to produce this
  object?
- Can we produce this locally?

- Can we produce this elsewhere?
- How do you choose where to produce this?
- What happens if you need it but cannot produce it locally?
- What are the pros and cons of producing this locally versus importing it?
- Do you think one is better than the other, and why?

Student Learning Objectives, Students Will be Able To:
- Know about one common resource that is imported and one resource that is produced locally
- Learn the specific conditions of production of at least one resource
- Name at least one nation or region with which their nation/region trades with

Assessment: Mind maps; their classroom discussion participation in the brainstorming and the debate.

Sequence of activities:

- **(5 min)** Teacher will present pictures of list of objects or resources and ask students to guess where they are produced. [Alternatively, if time allows, this can be a small group activity where one student tries to find out where an object is produced by reading the product label while other students in the group try to guess where the object is produced.]
- **(10 min)** Teacher will choose one imported resource, and demonstrate the use of a mind map by leading students through a whole-class brainstorming session to examine the pros and cons of importing the resource and producing it locally. The teacher will prompt students to consider the factors that exist in both their own nation/region, and the factors in the object's region of production.
- **(10 min)** Teacher then picks another resource, and students are then divided into small groups to produce a similar mind map on poster paper.
- **(15 min)** The mind maps produced by the small groups are displayed at the front of the classroom, and student groups are divided into two sides for debate: one side will argue that the resource is better imported, while the other side will argue that the resource is better produced locally. Students can draw their arguments from poster mind maps created by other groups.

- **(5 min)** To conclude the debate, the teacher will introduce the idea that nations and regions are invariably interrelated. Students will discuss as a class some pros and cons of the interdependence between regions.

Resources for students: World map or regional map for students to understand where the country of origin is.

Resources for teachers:

Teachers may choose one locally produced and one imported resource from the following list of suggestions:

- Water
- A fruit
- A vegetable
- Cooking oil/ a condiment
- Fuel
- A drink

- A processed food
- Clothing
- Building/construction material
- Pens
- A book
- An electrical appliance

Grade 4 Lesson 4

"World - SDGs and Actionable Steps"

Time Frame: 45 minutes | **Subjects:** Math |
Designer: Eva Flavia Martinez Orbegozo
Standards: No Poverty (SDG 1), Zero Hunger (SDG 2), Good Health and Well-Being (SDG 3), Quality Education (SDG 4), Gender Equality (SDG 5)

Summary and Rationale: Students will explore their position as citizens of the world by gaining key insight on world statistics and reflecting upon their role as world citizens and potential social changemakers.

Instructional Goals: Students will gain understanding of relevant statistics and data about the world they inhabit. They will make use of mathematical tools to discuss key topics such as world population, distribution of religions, education achievement. They will be asked to engage in self-reflection, critical thinking, group work and discussions.

Understanding Goals:
- Students will understand that statistics and math are tools to describe the world, to compare different realities and raise awareness of important issues.
- They will understand that knowledge about key global topics is fundamental to explore their relation to the world around them and to eventually take action to improve it.

Essential questions:
- Why are percentages important to describe the world?
- How can we use charts to compare different statistics?
- Are these data helpful to understand facts about the world? How do they make you feel? What are your thoughts about this global picture of the world?
- Does that change your ideas about the world and what you can do to change it for the better? Do you think statistics are helpful to convince people about the need to tackle certain topics and effect change?

Student Learning Objectives, Students Will be Able To:
- Use percentages and charts to discuss their feelings about certain world issues in small groups. They will have to individually write at least one sentence using a percentage that brings up an issue that is interesting, surprising or shocking for them and explain why.
- Use percentages and charts to describe key topics such as world population, distribution of religions, education achievement and create a group presentation about the main figures related to one of the SDGs.
- Reflect on the power of statistics to communicate sense of urgency and to encourage action. They will include this reflection in the conclusion of their presentation.

Assessment: Individual prompt questions and group presentations.

Sequence of activities:

- **Introduction (Feel):**
  - Watch the video "If the world was 100 people…" available here: http://www.100people.org

  - *If the video is not available, infographics can be created with the data from this website:*
    http://100people.org/statistics_100stats.php?section=statistics

  - **Prompting dialogue:**
    - The teacher asks students to discuss:
      - What are the numbers that call your attention?
      - What topics are they related to?

  - **Students discuss in pairs and write an individual reflection:**
    - On a piece of paper each student is asked to write one number that has caught his or her attention, the topic that the number relates to, and why they find it interesting, cool, shocking, unfair, important or otherwise.
    - Students can write more than one sentence if they have time, but it is important that they express the way the data makes them feel.
    - **The structure of the sentence would be:**

116

- o **"Out of 100 people, _____ people are _____."**
- o **" I find this_____because_____."**
  - ■ Then the teacher takes a few examples and writes percentages on the board.

- **Percentages (Think):**
  - o By using the numbers provided by students, the teacher translates them into percentages on the board. This will be one way to depict and talk about the information that stood out to the students.

  - o **Example:** 1 would be dying of starvation, 15 would be undernourished, 21 would be overweight → 1% would be dying of starvation, 15% would be undernourished, 21% would be overweight

  - o Working with a partner, students will exchange their sentences and translate the numbers into percentages. The pairs will discuss their reflections and write them down on their individual sheets of paper.

- **Charts (Think):**
  By using a set of number for one of the categories discussed in pairs, the teacher explains how to comparatively show those percentages in a block chart.

- **Presentations (Act):**
  - o Students work in groups around a set of data on one topic that is interesting for them (it can be simpler with only two percentages --e.g. 83 would be able to read and write; 17 would not, or more complicated comparisons can be made). They need to create a board including:
    - ■ Percentages
    - ■ Representation in a block chart (teacher can provide a piece of paper already including graduated axes, students will need to draw their charts there)
    - ■ A few bullet points on ideas they find important about those numbers. They could mention whether they feel they are signaling a problem, how they feel

about it, why that is a problem and/or how it could be solved.

o A few groups of students will present their boards to the classroom and share their reflections. All groups will hand in their presentation materials.

Resources for students: examples of percentages and charts created by the teacher on the blackboard, teacher guidance in making block charts.

Resources for teachers:
- 100 People: http://tiny.cc/G4L4R1

Grade 4 Lesson 5

"Tying it All Together - The Final Product"

Time Frame: 45 minutes | **Subjects:** Theater, Language |
Designer: Madhuri Dhariwal
Standards: Peace, Justice, and Strong Institutions (SDG 16)

Summary and Rationale: The students will use the knowledge and skills gained in the previous 4 lessons, and create a performing arts project that ties it all together. This will help to make the learning from different subjects interrelate.

Instructional Goal: The students will be able to connect their own identities to the larger world and see their role in promoting sustainable growth, along with recognizing larger world problems (through their understanding of the SDGs). They will also be able to express this through a self-written play, thus understanding about the expression of ideas through theatre.

Understanding:
- How to use theatre as a means of expression.
- How the self, community, nation and world are actually interconnected.
- The position/ role of an individual in promoting sustainable growth
- Where they are with relation to the rest of the world - geographically and historically

Essential Questions:
- What are the different means of expression? (writing, speaking, performing, various arts)
- Do your values help you understand the world differently?
- Are the resources we currently have in the world only for us?
- Should we care about world problems?

Student Learning Objectives (Students Will be Able To):

Objective	Conditions	Observable Skill or behavior	Assessment
Understand that there is a world out there, bigger than their own.	From lessons 3-4	Will show in their writing/ play	Can the student identify resources from the world?
Understand how their values relate to the world.	From lessons 1-4.	Will show in their writing/ play	Can the students talk about values in context to the world and solving a world problem?
Translate their ideas into a play	In small groups	Write the play	Does the content of the play reflect the ideas discussed in class and from lesson 1-4?
Work collaboratively	In small groups	Discuss ideas and then write parts of the play	Do the students help each other while working in the group? (it can look different for different groups.)

Assessment:

A few assessment tools that can help the teacher assess whether the intended objective of the lesson was achieved are:

- The play written by students (find attached a rubric for the play)
- The brainstorming session for the play will also show the teacher if the previous learning objectives have been met.
- A short survey/ questionnaire asking students indirectly about sustainable growth and their role in world problems (find attached an example for the same) - to be included in objective 1 mentioned above.

Since this is the culmination of the previous 4 lessons, assessment about the content of those lessons would already be conducted.

Sequence of activities:

Teacher will...	time	Student will...
a. Explain what the class objective (that the students are going to write a play, assimilating the information from the previous 4 lessons). Also, talk about the different mediums of expressing one's ideas and bring theatre as the one being used in this class.	5 minutes	(Try to) understand the objective. Will give their inputs about different mediums of expression.
b. Give an example of the play and an outline of what s/he wants them to do	5 minutes	Learn from the examples and ask questions if they don't understand the prompt.
c. Facilitate a brainstorming session for ideas on the play. Then with the students input, narrow down on one topic. (if there are too many students - maybe break it down to 2 groups and have them write different plays.)	10 minutes	Brainstorm ideas on what their play should look like, as a large group.
d. Assign parts of the play-writing to different students/ groups if the class is really large (it shouldn't be more than 5-10 lines per student, depending on the size of the class.) Division can be in different ways. One way could be diving the play into 4 acts, and assigning the acts to different groups and dividing the roles within the acts.	5 minutes	Get settled in their roles / groups.
e. Give the students time to write their part	20 minutes	Will write their sections
f. Collect the parts and put it together at home	1 minute	Will submit their parts
The teacher will collate and edit the play at home and share it with the students in the next class. They can then choose to perform it in class, or for the entire school or as a year-end showcase!		

Resources for students:
- Example of plays
- Notes from the previous 4 lessons. (summaries/ recap)

Resources for teachers:
- Example of plays: http://tiny.cc/G4L5R1

- Rubric:
  - 1. Does the content of the play reflect:
    - the values of the students
    - the values of sustainability
    - connections to the world
  - 2. Is the play
    - interesting to watch
    - easy to understand
    - clear in structure

Grade 5

Lesson Overview

Learning Goal

In Grade 5, students will learn about diversity, culture, and communication through the lens of religion. By learning about the role of religion in their own lives, communities, and across the world, students will come to appreciate the richness of cultural diversity. Students will also discuss how people can communicate across cultural differences, and come together to solve problems.

Lesson Scaffold	
Lesson 1	**How do My Values Relate to the Values of Others?**
Lesson 2	**What Does Religion Look Like in My Community?**
Lesson 3	**Religion Across the World**
Lesson 4	**Exploring Religion**
Lesson 5	**Communication, Conflict and Collaboration Across Religions.**
Learning Objectives	

- Students will learn about new cultures, focusing on the religions of the world.
- Students will think critically about the role of religion and other cultural institutions in their own community and lives.
- Students will use communication and problem-solving skills to develop ways to address conflict across differences.

Fernando M. Reimers et al.

Grade 5 Lesson 1

"How do My Values Relate to Others?"

Time Frame for each Lesson: 60 minutes | **Subjects::** Civics, History, Social Studies | **Designers:** Isabelle Byusa, Arianna Pattek, Emily Pope, Sam (Shiv) Sharma, Tisha Verma and Devon Wilson

Standards: Reduced Inequalities (SDG 10), Peace, Justice, and Strong Institutions (SDG 16), Quality Education (SDG 4)

Summary and Rationale: To enable students to explore the intersection of values and religion, , students will complete an exercise where they articulate their own values, and then discuss how different religions may or may not align with those values. In doing so, students will gain a greater understanding of why people believe and worship in different ways, as well as

Instructional Goal: Students will articular their values, and learn which religions may or may not align with their personal value set.

Understanding Goal: Cultivate tolerance for all religions, gain a deeper understanding of their own personal identity

Essential questions:
- What is religious tolerance?
- What is your religion and what does your religion value?
- How can we build tolerance and respect for religious diversity?

Student Learning Objectives, Students Will be Able To:
- Develop an awareness of religions around the world
- Develop an understanding of the overlap between religions' and their values
- Develop an appreciation and respect for religious diversity

Assessment: Students can demonstrate an understanding of their values and how they relate to the values of the class as a whole.

Sequence of Activities:

- **Pre Class:** Talk with students about values, and ask students to reflect on their values and pick the 5-10 values that are the most important to them.

- **Start:** Have students predict how similar their values are to other students. Have a discussion about how people's values are similar or different.

- **Next** list values placed in categories, and ask students which category they align with most and vote on that category.

- **Then** reveal to students what religion those values align with. (Veil of Ignorance type activity)

- **Transfer to religion** → discuss with students how values and religion from categories interrelate, and where they are different.

- **Local:** Discuss with students how religion exists in one's community?

- **Questions to explore and research on their own:**
  - How many religions exist in the world?
  - Watch the 100 video
  - Research the religion of one's ancestry.

Resources for students:

- 100 People Project: http://tiny.cc/G5L1R1

Resources for teachers:

- 100 People: http://tiny.cc/G5L1R2

Grade 5 Lesson 2

"What Does Religion Look Like in My Community"

Time Frame for each Lesson: 60 minutes | **Subjects::** Civics, History, Social Studies
Designers: Isabelle Byusa, Arianna Pattek, Emily Pope, Sam (Shiv) Sharma, Tisha Verma and Devon Wilson

Standards: Reduced Inequalities (SDG 10), Peace, Justice, and Strong Institutions (SDG 16), Quality Education (SDG 4)

Summary and Rationale: The goal of this lesson is to help students to become aware and reflect on their place in this world where many religions are practiced and find connections in their own local community.

Instructional Goals: Students will explore the religions present in their own community, and think about how these different religions interact with each other and the community at large.

Understanding Goals: Learn about the different religions present in their local community

Essential questions: Should a difference in religion even be a factor in how we view our local community members?

Student Learning Objectives, Students Will be Able To:
- Develop familiarity with different religions in the student's local community (or regional community)

Assessment: Students will be able to demonstrate an understanding of different religions present in their local community.

Sequence of Activities:
- Class discussion on different religions - reviewing content from prior lesson.

- Prompt students to split into groups to explore the religions available in one's community - either through accessing online resources such as websites and youtube videos or by having students walk around in their local community and visit different houses of worship (ideally students can visit and have first hand exposure to different religious sites).

- Class discussion in which students reflect on what they learnt about the different religions in their local community. Students can share 1-2 big ideas about they took from their topic - and 1-2 big ideas that they tool from others topics.

Resources for teachers:
- The United Nations Global Survey: http://tiny.cc/G5L2R1

Grade 5 Lesson 3

"Religion Across the World"

Time Frame for each Lesson: 60 minutes | **Subjects::** Civics, History, Social Studies

Designers: Isabelle Byusa, Arianna Pattek, Emily Pope, Sam (Shiv) Sharma, Tisha Verma and Devon Wilson

Standards: Reduced Inequalities (SDG 10), Peace, Justice, and Strong Institutions (SDG 16), Quality Education (SDG 4)

Summary and Rationale: To expose students to religious leaders who are making positive contributions to their societies, and spark a discussion by having them think of and articulate questions in a mindful, respectful manner while learning the similarities and differences between world religions.

Instructional Goal: Students will learn about a famous religious leader, and discuss what they have done to promote understanding and religions tolerance.

Understanding Goals: Cultivate tolerance for all religions, gain a deeper understanding of their own personal identity

Essential questions:
- What is religious tolerance?
- What is your religion and what does your religion value?
- Who are the leaders that represent religions of the world?
- How can we build tolerance and respect for religious diversity?

Student Learning Objectives, Students Will be Able To:
- Become familiar with world religions through religious leaders.
- Reflect on the similarities and differences in religion.
- Cultivate an appreciation for all people regardless of religion.

Assessment: An "Out of Respect and Curiosity Sheet" that highlights reflective questions students have of the religions they will have had the opportunity to explore.

Sequence of Activities:

- **Start (20 minutes)** by reviewing a list of world religions. Then, proceed to give an example of major and minor major religions, following giving an overview of:
    - Major beliefs of the religion
    - Sacred texts
    - Festivities and ceremonies
    - Clothing
- **Next, (for 25 minutes)** have students listen to a recording, watch a video, or read a text of a religious leader that has made positive contributions to society. Examples include Mahatma Gandhi, Martin Luther King Jr., Mother Teresa, Malala Yousafzai, Aga Khan or many others. A local religious leader in the community may work as an option. Prompt students to turn and talk to one another sharing what they have learned from these leaders, and comparing them to one another.
    - ***Question Prompts:***
        - How does religion play into social change?
        - How does religion influence leadership?
        - What are the differences and similarities between these leaders?
- Finally, in the last **15 minutes** of the class, ask students to reflect on the class by writing to a religious leader. The only guidelines for the students is that they must write out of curiosity and respect, to challenge students to write their questions in a sensitive and mindful manner. After the reflection exercise students will share their questions, and the instructor will affirm those students whose questions are mindful, and help those whose questions are insensitive by suggesting words that form their questions in a more mindful, neutral, curious way.

Resources for teachers:
- Religious Tolerance: http://tiny.cc/G5L3R1
- Teaching Tolerance: http://tiny.cc/G5L3R2
- Taking a Closer Look at Religions Around the World: http://tiny.cc/G5L3R3
- Teaching About Religion: http://tiny.cc/G5L3R4
- Maintain Neutrality: http://tiny.cc/G5L3R5

Grade 5 Lesson 4

"Exploring Religion"

Time Frame for each Lesson: 60 minutes | **Subjects::** Civics, History, Social Studies

Designers: Isabelle Byusa, Arianna Pattek, Emily Pope, Sam (Shiv) Sharma, Tisha Verma and Devon Wilson

Standards: Reduced Inequalities (SDG 10), Peace, Justice, and Strong Institutions (SDG 16), Quality Education (SDG 4)

Summary and Rationale: Students will be given a class period to start on a miniature group research project where they can explore a religious topic they are curious about - and will share their research and discovery with other students. Students should be encouraged to select a topic they are less familiar with - ideally the topic will not be broadly related to their own religion if they actively practice.

Instructional Goals: Students will research a new topic about religion and share their findings with other students.

Understanding Goals: Cultivate fact-based tolerance for all religions.

Essential questions:
- What are you curious about?
- How can we explore and share what we learn?

Student Learning Objectives Students Will be Able To:
- Develop a deeper understanding of and awareness of religions.
- Develop research, writing and editing skills.

Assessment: The final product after students receive revisions and feedback from the newspaper editor (either the teacher or a student in class)

Sequence of Activities:
- **Part 1**
  - Students will first be asked 'How are newspapers made?' This will hopefully lead to a discussion about reporters, and research techniques.

131

- o From here, teachers will ask students what is important to consider as a reporter (accuracy; writing in a way that interests people; the effect on the public, etc.)
- o Here it will be introduced that the class is planning to open a school newspaper. To make this happen, there are different positions that need to be filled (newspaper designer, newspaper editors, etc.) and students will be challenged to take on these roles as well as serving as reporters.

- **Part 2**
  - o Students will be asked what religions would be interesting to report on: religions will be taken and written on the board. Students will then be asked what are we curious about involving these religions and subcategories will be created. e.g. (history, locations around the world, the different hierarchical positions, relation to one's own community, values, holidays, what famous people practice that religion, etc.).
  - o Students will be encouraged to come up to the board and put their names by projects of interest, or create new topics that they would like to research in the realm of religion.

- **Part 3**
  - o Students will be challenged to develop a research plan on their own in pairs including:
    - A few questions/things the student is curious about the topic.
    - Reflection and documentation on what students currently know about the topic.
  - o Students will be given the rest of the period to start their research for their first draft article due in one week*.

- **Part 4**
  - o Once drafts are completed, students will be given peer "editor" feedback on the topics of: was the reporting unbiased/did it attract the reader's attention/was it free of grammatical errors, etc. Then students will be given a chance to make revisions before their piece goes to the final editor (the teacher).

132

- **Part 5**
  - ○ From here, either the teacher can piece the articles together and share them with students, or an additional activity can be created where students come up with a newspaper name, and think and experiment with different designs for editing the available pieces (either online via a blog; or through print).

- **Part 6**
  - ○ Once the project is completed, students will be asked to go back to their initial notes and answer the following reflection question: "I used to think _____." "I know know _____." (See Visible Thinking Framework link below for more info on this activity.)

Resources for teachers:
- Visible Thinking Framework – Project Zero: http://tiny.cc/G5L4R1

Grade 5 Lesson 5

"Communication, Conflict, and Collaboration Across Religions"

Time Frame for each Lesson: 60 minutes | **Subjects::** Civics, History, Social Studies
Designers: Isabelle Byusa, Arianna Pattek, Emily Pope, Sam (Shiv) Sharma, Tisha Verma and Devon Wilson

Standards: Reduced Inequalities (SDG 10), Peace, Justice, and Strong Institutions (SDG 16), Quality Education (SDG 4)

Summary and Rationale: To utilize knowledge from previous lessons and apply it to a real-life scenario.

Instructional Goal: Students will discuss religious intolerance in the context of a hypothetical scenario, and consider how this translates to their lives.

Understanding Goal: How to work across differences, how to identify a problem, how to reach consensus on a peaceful solution that includes the viewpoints of all parties involved.

Essential questions: What is conflict? How do we resolve problems peacefully?

Student Learning Objectives, Students Will be Able To:
- Present an inclusive solution (measurable by class participation: present in front of the group)
- Work productively in a group setting (measurable through teacher observations of group work and student reflection of group process)

Assessment: Rubric for the group presentation drawn from regional or common core standards for speaking and listening, for grade 5.

Sequence of Activities:

- **Pre-class (10 min):** Ask the class the following questions to open with a class discussion, begin in small groups then open to full class:
  - What does conflict mean?

135

    o   What does intolerance mean to you?

    o   When was a time you have witnessed a conflict? What happened?

    o   What feelings/emotions did you observe in each party of the conflict?

    o   How did they come to a solution?

- **Main activity (30 min):**

Split students into groups of no more than 4-5 students. Read the scenario to the whole class, then allow them time to work in small groups to design a skit that models their ideal solution.

In the country of Zorg, there are 4 main national religions. The majority of people belong to the religion of Tor. The other three religions are Zaria, Mooka, and Bic. Tor and Zaria fundamentally oppose the idea of girls going to school based on their religious doctrine. Mooka and Bic both believe girls have a right to attend school given to them by their god. Additionally, Zaria, Mooka, and Bic don't feel represented in the government, as it is dominated by people from the Tor religion. The government is trying to pass a law to prevent girls from attending school because of their religion. Mooka, Bic, and Zaria are resorting to violent protests in the capital of Zorg to have their voices heard. This only makes Tor more unwilling to negotiate with the other religions. What do you do?

- **Presentation and conclusion (20 min):** Students present their solutions in skits of 3-4 minutes each. Teacher leads a discussion on personal reflection of the process. What went well? What did you learn?

Resources for students:
- Resolving Conflict Situations: http://tiny.cc/G5L5R1

Resources for teachers:
- Standards for Speaking and Listening: http://tiny.cc/G5L5R2

Grade 6

Lesson Overview
Learning Goal
In previous grades, students have explored what it means to be a part of a community, identified ways that they can contribute to the well-being of that community, learned about the value of diversity within communities, and gained tools for connecting with people across difference. In grade 6, students will be adopt a critical lens towards these concepts of community and begin to explore how privilege, inequality, power dynamics, and social justice play into their own lives.

Lesson Scaffold	
Lesson 1	**Personal Identity, Privilege, and Inequality**
Lesson 2	**My Place in the Community**
Lesson 3	**My Place in the Nation**
Lesson 4	**My Place in the World**
Lesson 5	**Making Changes in My Daily Life**

Learning Objectives
<ul><li>Students will explore the various facets of their own privilege and that of others.</li><li>Students will identify potential historical, social, or cultural factors that may have given rise to that privilege.</li><li>Students will understand how others' identities, privilege, and experiences differ from their own, and take steps to address inequality in their own lives.</li></ul>

Grade 6 Lesson 1

"Personal Identity, Privilege, and Inequality"

Time Frame: 60 minutes | **Subjects:** Humanities, Social Studies

Designers: Somoh Supharukchinda (with Alexandra Ball, Deaweh Benson, Heer Shaikh, and Nicolas Riveros)

Standards: No Poverty (SDG 1); Quality Education (SDG 4); Gender Equality (SGG 5); Reduced Inequalities (SDG 10); Decent Work and Economic Growth (SDG 8); Peace, Justice, and Strong Institutions (SDG 16)

Summary and Rationale:

- This lesson aims to help students discuss and reflect on their personal identities and the factors that shape their identities. Students will begin to consider how these identities may differ from others and the ways in which aspects of identity may create inequalities and/or grant certain people privilege.
- Two key exercises will serve as starting points for discussion and reflection. In the first exercise, students will participate in a game that simulates how an individual's position may impact their opportunities and success in life. In the second exercise, students will dig into their own identity by creating an "identity wheel" and making connections to how the components of their identity may impact their privilege and place in society.

Instructional Goals (Competencies):

- Knowledge and Skills
  - Understand one's own identity and roots, others' identities and roots, how cultures shape identities, and where one is situated in space and time (Self-Awareness)
  - Understand how values are created through culture, religion, and experience

139

- o Students will be able to question the existing power structures and be aware of their place within a specific world context
- Ethical and Intercultural Orientation
    - o Cultivate an appreciation, curiosity, and respect for cultural diversity and world culture as the foundation for both self-reflection and an empathetic approach to human interaction.
    - o Belief of basic equality of all people and their potentials

Understanding Goals: My background and experiences shape my identity, as well as the opportunities that I can access. Others' backgrounds and experiences differ, and some of these differences can create inequalities and influence my level of privilege in the world.

Essential questions:
- What factors shape our identities and those of others?
- How do the different factors that shape our identities impact the opportunities we have access to?
- Are these differences fair? Why or why not?

Student Learning Objectives, Students Will be Able To:
- Articulate the main components of their identities.
- Describe how the components that make up their identities may differ from those of others.
- Explain how identities may impact the opportunities people can access and what privileges these afford them (or not).

Assessment: (Optional Homework) Students will write a brief journal on their reflections from the personal identity exercises and share two examples they see of how differences in identity may influence opportunities they or others can access.

Sequence of Activities:
- **Introduce lesson (1 min):** Explain that the purpose of the lesson to explore our identities, what makes up our identities, how they might differ from others, and how this impacts the opportunities we can access. If students are unfamiliar with the terminology, define identity as "a way you define yourself."
- **Conduct inequality activity (9 mins):**
    - o As students enter the classroom, they are assigned to seats. Each seat has a crumpled piece of paper. Instruct students

that they have a chance to win a prize. To win a prize, they must remain in their seats and toss their paper into the "basket" (a trash can) at the front of the room. Students should be seated such that certain seats are clearly advantageous. Those students that make a basket receive a prize (e.g., candy, chocolate, etc.) Modifications: Students who make a basket receive another crumpled ball for extra shots at more prizes.

- **Facilitate debrief/discussion (14 mins)**
  - ○ Have students discuss the number of prizes they got, who got the prizes, and how they felt. If students do not express any feelings of frustration or concern, prompt them to discuss if they thought the activity was fair. Could the students in front have helped out the students in the back (e.g., by sharing their additional sheets of paper)? Share that this activity was intended to simulate real life disparities. What connections do they see? What if the candy was money, schools, jobs, etc.? What factors in real life might lead someone to end up in the front row rather than the back row?

- **Conduct personal identity wheel activity (18 mins)**
  - ○ Share that the class will now engage in an activity that allows them to more deeply explore these questions of identity. First, you will model an identity wheel as a circular graphic with pieces representing each aspects of your identity-- for example, your name, gender, race, job, position in your family, etc. The size of the slices should correspond to how much that particular aspect contributes to your identity (larger slices mean that aspect is a larger part of your identity). Share with students why you selected the aspects you did and why you sized them as you did.
  - ○ Instruct students to create their own identity wheel based on what they think is important to their identity. They should each have a piece of paper and markers/coloring pencils/writing utensils. You could prompt them to consider:
    - ■ Geography (country, city, village, etc.)
    - ■ Gender
    - ■ Race/ethnicity/tribe/etc.
    - ■ Religion

■ Family relationships (daughter, son, brother, etc.)

- **Share and discuss identity wheels (10 mins)**
  - ○ In groups of 3-4, have students share their completed identity wheels with each other, sharing their rationale for why they selected the aspects and sizes they did.

- **Conclusion (8 mins)**
  - ○ Have students share out: What identities were they most aware of? Did they think about some more than others? Did this differ from their classmates? Were they surprised by anything they saw in their classmates' identity wheels? Why or why not? How might these relate to the first activity?

Resources for teachers:
- An effective lesson about privilege: http://tiny.cc/G6L1R1
- Description of the paper and trash can lesson: http://tiny.cc/G6L1R2
- An example of a personal identity wheel: http://tiny.cc/G6L1R3

Grade 6 Lesson 2

"My Place in the Community"

Time Frame: 60 minutes | **Subjects**: Social Studies, English, Civics | **Designer**: Alexandra Ball

Standards: No Poverty (SDG 1); Reduced Inequalities (SDG 10); Sustainable Cities and Communities (SDG 11); Peace , Justice and Strong Institutions

Summary and Rationale:

- In this lesson, students will extend their understandings of privilege and identity covered in Lesson 1 to the community level. Students will begin by recalling the identity wheels they created in the previous lesson; this will serve as a starting point for a brief discussion of how different aspects of a person's identity can affect their privilege and opportunities.

- Next, you will lead the students in an exploration of how inequality can affect people living in the same community, using the specific example of income equality. Students will embark on a guided thought experiment on how two people with different levels of income may have very different lives and experiences, despite belonging to the same community. Students will reflect on this experience with a 5-minute quick write exercise, which they will then share in small groups.

- The class will reconvene with a whole class discussion in which students will share their thoughts on the exercise, and brainstorm ways in which Townville could promote equality.

Instructional Goal: To lead students in a thought experiment on the influence of inequality within communities.

Understanding Goal: Even within individual communities, people may have differing levels of privilege, different experiences, and different capabilities. I must be aware of these dynamics at work within my own community, and start to think how equality of opportunity can be promoted at a local level.

143

Essential questions:
- Are all members of a community automatically the same? Why or why not?
- What are the consequences of inequality at the local level?
- What can communities do to make sure that all people have the same freedoms and opportunities?

Student Learning Objectives, Students Will be Able To:
- Apply previous learnings to both hypothetical and real-life scenarios.
- Think critically about that which they observe in their everyday lives.
- Demonstrate creativity in solving social problems.

Assessment:
At the end of class, each student will submit one suggestion for addressing income inequality on the local level (in the context of the activity)

Sequence of Activities:
- **Introduction/Defining Terms (5 minutes):**
  - You will explain that students will be exploring inequality as it exists within a given community. You should then ask the class what they think a community, and, using student suggestions, write a class definition for "community" on the board. (This definition may describe a neighborhood, town, village, school, or city; the broadness is left up to your discretion.)

- **Framing/Lesson 1 Recap (5 minutes):**
  - You will ask students to recall their identity maps from the last class. Then, you will have students turn and talk with their classmates about the different sources of identity variation that they identified through their maps.
  - You should circulate for about three minutes, listening to student discussions and prompting them to think of more factors that may shape someone's identity.

- **Introduction to Kidville (10 minutes):**
  - After reconvening the class, you will introduce the students to "Townville," a fictional community. You will draw a simple map of Townville on the board, identifying features such as a schools, markets, roads, downtown areas, geographical features, town hall, etc.

- ○ Next, you will draw two houses on the board: Circle House and Square House. These houses are next-door neighbors in Townville; both house a family with a mother, father, and one child. The only difference is that the yearly income of Circle House is 100 Townbucks, while the income of Square House is 50 Townbucks.

- You will then explain that the students are going to see what it would be like to live in each house.

- **Activity Set up (5 minutes):**
  - ○ You then break the class in half: one side will represent Circle House, and the other will represent Square House.
  - ○ Within their halves, students should get into groups of 3-4. As they do, you will pass out Townbucks to every group-- Circle House groups will get 10 Townbucks, and Square House groups will get 5 Townbucks. (You should cut out enough bills ahead of time.)

- **Activity (10 minutes):**
  - ○ Once students are in groups and have their money, you will write a series of activities on the board, each with a different price (the amounts should be in increments of 10, up to 50 Townbucks). The tasks should be activities typical to 6th graders in the context in which the lesson is being implemented (i.e. playing, drawing, reading, etc)
  - ○ You will then explain that these Townbucks represent how much money that child has saved up; now, each group will have to decide what they want to spend their money on and why. (The complexity of this activity is again left up to you-- it can be as simple as a list of items, or a sequences of activities with subcosts).

- **Reconvening/Discussion (10 minutes):**
  - ○ After 10 minutes of group discussion, you will first ask each Circle House Group what they spent their money on, and then each Square House group what they spent their money on.
  - ○ You will then lead the class in a discussion comparing the choices of the two sides of the room, prompting the students to discuss if they found this unfair and why. (It may be most

productive for you to play devil's advocate, saying things like, "But these kids had access to all the same things and live right next door. What's unfair about that?")

- **In our own community (10 minutes):**
  - You will then ask students to take out a piece of paper and to do a 5-minute free write about how this activity applies to their own community. During this time, you should circulate around the room and may prompt struggling students with questions such as, "How would it feel to live in the Square House?" or "Can you think of any ways other than income that families in the same community may be different from each other?"
  - After 5 minutes, you may ask students to share their thoughts. (Note: you will have to moderate this discussion carefully, as students will be talking about their own communities and may breach some sensitive and/or personal topics).
- **Wrap up (5 minutes):**
  - If there is time, you should ask students what they think could be done to ensure that the child from the Square House has all the same opportunities as the child from the Circle House. After class brainstorming, each student should write down one suggestion, which can serve as their exit-ticket.

Resources for teachers:
- Dollar Design: http://tiny.cc/G6L2R1

Grade 6 Lesson 3

"My Place in the Nation"

Time Frame: 45 minutes | **Subjects:** History, Social Studies, Language Arts

Designers: Alexandra Ball, Heer Shaikh, Deaweh Benson, Somoh Supharukchinda

Standards: Reduced Inequalities (SDG 10); Peace, Justice and Strong Institutions (SDG 16); Partnerships for the Goals (SDG 17)

Summary and Rationale:
- In this lesson, students will discuss inequality in a national context, having already begun to explore their personal identity/place in the community. Specifically, they will be pushed to consider how their experiences compare to those of others in their country, how they may be different, and why.
- This will be accomplished through a "choose-your-own-adventure" style creative writing/performance exercise. Students will be "introduced" to three children, all hailing from different communities/regions/cultures within their country. After being given some basic facts about that child's life, students will be broken into groups and asked to imagine/present different stages of that child's life. After presenting to the group, students will debrief about how these children's experiences differed from their own and reasons for those differences.

Instructional Goals:

- To guide the students in imagining what life would be like for other people in their national context.
- *Note: in order to make this lesson applicable in different cultural contexts, you should create three child profiles prior to the lesson. These profiles should contain basic information about the fictional child (name, where they are from, family, if they live in an urban/rural setting, religion, or any other details that may be relevant

to the exercise). In order for the lesson to be successful, however, these profiles must be fundamentally different from each other.

Understanding Goals: Even within my country, people of different regions/communities/cultures have different experiences and opportunities than I do.

Essential Questions:

- How do these experiences/identities of others within my own country differ from my own?
- What are the reasons why these experiences differ?
- How do these differences influence our opportunities/life trajectories?

Student Learning Objectives, Students Will be Able To:
- Read/understand descriptions of their characters.
- Create/present a representation of their characters at ages 11, 16, and 21
- Engage with a discussion of how these characters' experiences at each age differ, why these differences exist, and the significance of these differences.

Assessment:

- Although there is no formal assessment, the teacher should make sure that each student is engaging with their group activities, and participates in the eventual presentation of their group's story.
- Each student should turn in a one-sentence summary of something they learned (as an exit ticket).

Sequence of Activities:

- **Introduction (10 minutes)**
  - Students are presented with a sample "story" of a typical student from their own community-- introduction to the student and brief descriptions of the student's life/community/family.
  - Students are then presented with brief bios of three more students, each from different cultures/regions/communities within their country, and given instructions to imagine how

those students' lives might differ from their own, and why. During these instructions, you should provide prompts such as: "Would this student go to a school like this?" "What do you think this student likes to do for fun?"

- **Activity Set-up (2 minutes)**
  - ○ Students are broken into groups of 4-5 students, each assigned to one of the fictional students. Multiple groups can be assigned the same student.
- **Activity (10-15 minutes)**
  - ○ In groups, students will tell the story of their fictional student. Student can choose the manner in which they want to express their story (writing, performance, art, etc.). You should have a variety of materials available for students to use if they wish.
- **Presentation (10 minutes)**
  - ○ Each group will present their fictional student's story to the class.

- **Discussion (10 minutes)**
  - ○ After students have finished presenting, you should lead the class in a discussion of how all the stories were different, even though they all took place in the same country. You should then push students to consider the ways in which the stories were similar.

- **Wrap up/Exit Ticket (2 minutes)**
  - ○ Before the end of class, each student should write down one thing that surprised them about the exercise.

Resources for teachers:
Examples of creative ways to present children's stories: http://tiny.cc/G6L3R1
Example of a Comic Strip: http://tiny.cc/G6L3R2
A template to organize their child's information (however, students should only use this as a planning tool): http://tiny.cc/G6L3R3

Grade 6 Lesson 4

"My Place in the World"

Time Frame: 45 minutes | **Subjects:** Geography, Civics

Standards: No Poverty (SDG 1), Quality Education (SDG 4), Reduce Inequality (SDG 10), Peace Justice and Strong Institutions (SDG 16)

Designers: Alexandra Ball, Heer Shaikh, Deaweh Benson, Somoh Supharukchinda

Summary and Rationale: In this lesson students will be exposed to the global inequalities in order to increase their awareness and sensitivity of their role as global citizens. This will go hand in hand with the themes in the framework of cultivating an appreciation, curiosity, and respect for cultural diversity and world culture as the foundation for self-reflection, identity formation, and empathetically approaching human interaction. Students should recognize and appreciate the interdependence of all people, living things, and the planet.

Instructional Goal: This lesson will exposure students to global statistics and disparities, and encourage them to consider their own personal responsibility.

Understanding Goals: Students will understand how global inequality affects the way that countries interact with each other, and gain useful problem-solving skills.

Essential Questions:
- What makes countries different from each other?
- How do these differences affect their interactions?
- How do these global interactions impact individual people's lives?

Student Learning Objectives (Students Will be Able To):
- Put themselves in another's shoes and think critically about their actions.
- Practice problem-solving and collaboration with classmates.
- Understand how conflicts play out on a global level.

Activities:

- **Introduction (5 minutes)**
  - o You will ask students to recall the last two lessons, where they explored issues of inequality and diversity on a community and national level. Then, you will explain that today, the students will be applying those same lessons to the global level through a United Nations (UN) simulation.
  - o You will briefly describe what the UN is and how countries send representatives there to negotiate on behalf of the whole country. You may want to show students the UN website or other media on the UN, if time and resources permit.

- **Activity Set up (10 minutes)**
  - o You will explain that the students will be role-playing different countries. To do so, you should break the class into groups of 4-5 students. Each group will then be assigned a country. (The countries should represent a range of sizes, regions, ethnicities, and economies).
  - o Once all groups have been assigned a country, you will reconvene the class and pose a problem for the class to solve. This problem is left up to your discretion, but it would be most useful it is was something about which the students had some level of awareness, or something relevant to the community in which this lesson is being taught. Possible problems might include: a war between two countries in the room, a regional water/resource shortage, a problem in another country, etc.
  - o You should then distribute to each group a sheet of paper detailing their country's stance on the problem (to be prepared ahead of time). This should include information on the opinions of the country's populations/leaders, any economic/resource-based stakes in the problem, and any influence/bargaining chips the country has with other countries in the simulation).

- **Activity (15 minutes)**
  - o When you say, the students will break into their groups and attempt to come to a consensus decision on how to solve the

problem. This time should be left relatively unstructured, with students free to strategize within their own groups, or negotiate with other groups.

- o During this time, you should circulate to facilitate negotiations. You should make sure that all groups consider what strategies would be in their own best interests and how those interests may differ from other countries' interests.

- **Reconvening (10 minutes)**
  - o You will call the class back together and have the class collectively present their solution (if they were able to arrive at one).
  - o You will then lead the class in a discussion of the activity, prompting them to talk about:
    - Was it difficult to agree with countries that were different from your own? Why?
    - How did you protect your own interests when negotiating?
    - Did certain countries in the class have more power than other countries? Why?
    - Was this a fair process? Why or why not?

Resources:
- Information for Country Profiles: http://tiny.cc/G6L4R1
- Sample UN Mini-Simulations: http://tiny.cc/G6L4R2
- Model UN Mini- Simulations: http://tiny.cc/G6L4R3
- Model UN - Lesson 13 Manual: http://tiny.cc/G6L4R4

Grade 6 Lesson 5

"Making Changes in My Daily Life"

Time Frame: 45 minutes | **Subjects**: Social Studies, Civics, Art |
Designer: Alexandra Ball
Standards: No Poverty (SDG 1), Quality Education (SDG 4), Reduce
Inequality (SDG 10), Peace Justice and Strong Institutions (SDG 16)

Summary and Rationale:
In this lesson, students will bring their focus back to the local level, picking an
issue they want to support within their own community. This issue could be
anything that piques the students' individual interests-- environmental
protection, hunger, homelessness, racial inequalities, etc. During this lesson,
they will develop a list of five things they can do to address this issue in their
everyday lives. They will then make posters of these five steps, which will be
displayed around the school/classroom.

Instructional Goal: Identify issues of inequity/need within their own
communities and empower students to take personal steps to address issues
of personal interest to them.

Understanding Goals: I must apply a critical lens to what I see happening
every day in my community. I have the capability and the power to make a
difference, and I have the responsibility to try.

Essential questions: How do the issues of inequity, privilege, and justice
apply to my own community? What can I do to solve these issues, if I'm only
in 6th grade?

Student Learning Objectives (Students Will be Able To):
- Identify an issue of personal interest to them and pressing need in the
  community.
- Develop a list of five ways to address that issue.
- Present list to the class.

Assessment: Completed poster with five action steps, to be turned in at the
end of class.

Sequence of Activities:
- **Introduction (5 minutes)**:
  - ○ You will recap the issues students have explored in the last four lessons: personal privilege/identity, as well as the reality and consequences of inequality at the local, national, and global levels.
  - ○ After students have named some of the issues they have discussed, you should write this quote on the board: "Never doubt that a small group of thoughtful, committed citizens can change the world; indeed, it's the only thing that ever has." - Margaret Mead
  - ○ You should ask the students what they think this quote means, and whether they think they are capable of changing the world.
- **Instructions (5 minutes)**:
  - ○ You will explain that today, the students are going to be choosing an problem they see happening in their own community, and come up with a list of five ways to address it-- called "action steps."
  - ○ You may take suggestions of problems, or name a few examples. You should also provide a pile of local newspapers for students to look at if they can't think of any ideas.
- **Independent Work (25 minutes)**:
  - ○ The bulk of this lesson will be devoted to individual work time as students pick their issue and come up with steps they can take. If students want to focus on the same issue, they may work together in small groups.
  - ○ During this time, you should circulate continuously to help students identify relevant issues and think of creative action steps. You should encourage students to draw from their own experiences in the community and also to think about feasibility when developing their action steps (e.g., a 6th grader might not be able to start their own organization, but they can try to raise money to donate to a local NGO).
  - ○ At the end of this time, each student/group should have produced a small poster that names the problem they are addressing along with five action steps. If they have time, the students can decorate the posters with any available crayons, markers, stickers, etc.
  - ○

- **Presentations (10 minutes)**
  - For the last part of class, each student will share the issue they have chosen and their action items with the class. These should be displayed for the students to see, so that they can be continuously inspired to work for the good of the community.

Grade 7

Lesson Overview	
Learning Goal	
Having studied their role in their communities and the world at large, students will now start to conceptualize themselves as change-makers. By learning from their peers and other members of the community, students will begin to make plans for how they can make the world around them a better place.	
Lesson Scaffold	
Lesson 1	What SDG-related problems exist in my own country?
Lesson 2	How have other people solved these problems?
Lesson 3	How can I learn from other change-makers?
Lesson 4	What I have learned from other change-makers.
Lesson 5	What can we do now?
Learning Objectives	
• Students will practice research methods such as interviewing, analyzing information, and presenting findings. • Students will work in teams to creatively solve problems. • Students will exercise leadership, empathy, and agency.	

Grade 7 Lesson 1

"SDGs in our lives"

Time Frame: 60 minutes | **Subjects:** Social Studies, Science, Agriculture
Designer: Kara Howard

Standards: Lesson can be applicable to all 17 Sustainable Development Goals, depending on the issues the students see in their community contexts.

Summary and Rationale: This lesson aims to situate the Sustainable Development Goals into the lived experiences of students. Students will begin to perceive the problems they see in their communities within broader global problems.

Instructional Goals:
- Students will develop competencies that allow them to:
- Understand the rights of all humans to lead happy, healthy, and productive lives regardless of gender, age, disability, etc. (no poverty, no hunger, etc),
- Recognize and appreciate the interdependence of all people, living things, and the planet
- Be aware of the scarcity of water, energy, and food.
- Forge an ethical orientation towards our natural resources and all other forms of life - on land and water - and understand our responsibility to preserve/conserve our planet for sustainability.
- Analyze and researching solutions to problems (water, energy, and food) from the perspectives of different roles, such as consumers, businesses, scientists, policy makers, researchers, retailers, media, and development cooperation agencies, among others
- Believe that improvements can be made through growth mindset

Understanding Goals: Students will be able to see a connection between the problems their communities face and the larger global issues that the Sustainable Development Goals are aiming to address.

Essential questions:
- What are the enduring problems we see in our community?
- How do these problems fit within a broader global framework?
- Why do you think these problems exist in our society and in the world?

Student Learning Objectives (Students Will be Able To):
- Identify salient problems in their communities
- Connect these problems to those addressed by the Sustainable Development Goals
- Discuss why these problems exist in their communities

Assessment: Teacher will do informal assessments to ensure that students are thinking critically about the problems they brainstorm, directly giving the evidence they see of the problem, and why they think the problem exists in their community. If the teacher thinks a formal assessment is necessary, he/she could do an assessment where students are asked to connect their brainstormed problems to the Sustainable Development Goals.

Sequence of Activities:

- **Introduction:** Teacher will introduce the Sustainable Development goals to students. Teacher will explain that the goals we set to determine an agenda for where to focus efforts to improve our world by 2030. The teacher will write the 17 goals down - or have a teaching aid with them already written - and ask students to discuss whether they think these goals are important.

- **Sustainable Development Goals:**

No Poverty

Zero Hunger

Good Health and Well-Being

Quality Education

Gender Equality

Clean Water and Sanitation

Partnerships for the Goals

Affordable and Clean Energy

Life on Land

Decent Work and Economic Growth

Peace, Justice and Strong Institutions

Industry, Innovation, and Infrastructure

Reduced Inequalities

Sustainable Cities and Communities

Responsible Consumption and Production

Climate Action

Life Below Water

- **Activities:** With these goals in mind, students will break into small groups to discuss the problems they see in their own communities. Students should create lists of the problems they've identified along with the evidence they see that the problem exists. Students should also begin to develop a theory for why they think the problem exists in their community. Teacher should rotate between the groups assisting in developing their problem theories and helping them make connections to the Sustainable Development Goals.

- **Conclusion:** The small groups of students should then present their list of problems to the larger class. If time permits, the students can then discuss as a large group the problems they feel are most pressing to them.

Grade 7 Lesson 2

"Change Makers - Research People in the Community who are the Change Makers"

Time Frame: 60 minutes | **Subjects:** ELA, social studies | **Designer:** Chloé Suberville

Standards: Partnerships for the Goals (SDG 17), Reduced Inequalities (SDG 10), however lesson can be applicable to all 17 Sustainable Development Goals, depending on the issues the students see in their community contexts.

Summary and Rationale: This lesson aims to make students identify people in their community who are already making strides towards change in the problems they identified in the previous lesson.

Instruction Goal: Students will have made a list of people they know or have heard about in their communities who have made change in their community so that they have role models to interview, as a foundational step towards becoming agents of change in their own towns, state, country.

Understanding Goals: Students will be able to understand what makes a person a change maker and link that idea to people in their community.

Essential questions:
- What makes people agents of change?
- How do we know the type of change that they are making?
- Who are agents of change we know from around the world?
- What about in our communities?

Student Learning Objectives (Students Will be Able To):
- Understand what makes someone an agent of change
- Know what types of change an individual could be working on
- Look at people in their lives and identify the type of change they are striving for, on a small and large scale.

Assessment: Students have successfully identified at least one person in the community they will contact in order to identify as agents of change in their community, and that they may interview.

Sequence of Activities:
- Remind students that an agent of change can look a lot of different ways. Think about the previous lesson and the ways in which we identified the problems in our community. Tell the students we will be thinking of agents of change in the world but also in our communities so that we can contact them and use them as role models.
- Students will turn and talk to a partner about a time when they have seen people in their lives be agents of change, and react in an admirable way in certain situations. Remind the student that it can be someone from school, a friend, or neighbor. The teacher should walk around as students are talking and take notes on a few common themes that are being discussed. Bring the class together and have a few partners share what they discussed. Talk about the different themes that you have observed and tie them into the new themes students discussed with the class.
- Give students the attached graphic organizer and tell them to fill it out using someone they personally know (not a celebrity, but someone in their life).
- Students could take the graphic organizer home and talk through the answers with a role model, or someone they think might be an agent of change in their community so that they can start thinking about this with them.
- When in class students can work in groups of 3 and discuss their answers. Other students should give "hot and cold" feed back, tell them what is great with their graphic organizer and one thing that they can think about to improve it.
- After the graphic organizer has been completed, students will write a descriptive piece using the information they collected with the graphic organizer. Then, they can get back with their groups of 3 and have partners offer suggestions.
- Place the final drafts around the room and have students read each other's work. Bring the classroom together to discuss these questions:
  Debrief:
  - What themes repeatedly came up in your classmate's' writing?

166

- o   What are some similarities between the personal change agents your classmates described and the historical figures you know about?
- o   What are some differences?
- o   What did you learn from this activity about what motivates people to work for change and how
- o   they go about doing it?

Resources for Teachers:
- Role Model Graphic Organizer: http://tiny.cc/G7L2R1
- Change Agents in Our Own Lives: http://tiny.cc/G7L2R2

Grade 7 Lesson 3
" Interviewing and asking questions"

Time Frame: 60 minutes | **Subjects:** Social Studies, Civic Education | **Designer:** Nicolás Buchbinder

Standards: Peace, Justice, and Strong Institutions (SDG 16). Other goals could be included, depending on the specific interest of the students and the community they live in.

Summary and rationale: Students will learn about how to conduct an interview aiming to conduct their own interviews to change-makers in their communities.

Instructional Goals: Students will address how to conduct an interview to obtain valuable information on how to change society.

Understanding Goals: Students will learn to interview a change maker in their communities as part of the process of understanding how people make change in society. Students will focus in this class on what questions to ask and how to perform an interview.

Essential questions: What are important questions to ask a change maker in my community? How do I prioritize important questions?

Student Learning Objectives (Students Will be Able To):

- Engage in thinking questions to ask changemakers in their community.
- Practice and get feedback on how to do an interview.
- Create a protocol for an interview.

Assessment: Teacher will encourage participation as an informal way of assessing every student; teacher will collect the protocols created by students.

Sequence of Activities:

- **Opener: (5 minutes)** recalling what happened in the last class. Teacher will ask students to remember the activities performed in the last class. They will bring different community actors identified as change makers.

- **Activity #1: (10 minutes) Contacting the interviewee**
  Teacher should ask the entire group of students how would they contact a changemaker. They will go to different ways of doing that: emails, telephone or personal contact, etc. The class will agree on which is the best way to contact the interviewees for the project, and teacher will make a point on good manners when approaching them.

- **Activity #2: (15 minutes) The questions**
  Teacher will divide the students into different groups. Each of them will think 10 questions they want to ask to change makers in their communities. After that, the class as a whole will debrief different important questions and teacher will organize those in different important categories (personal background of the interviewee, area of concern, mobilizing efforts, obstacles for social change, results of activities, etc.).

- **Activity #3: (20 minutes) The practice of the interview**
  Teacher will simulate to be an interviewee and choose a couple of students to interview them. They will go through some questions agreed on Activity #2. After 5 minutes, the class will debrief on that experience, and talk about dividing roles in the interview and preparation materials (notes, recording, listening carefully, follow-up questions). After that, teacher will choose other two students and will perform again, this time acting as a "hostile" interviewee (one that does not talk much, talks about something different to the questions asked, etc.). After 5 minutes, teacher will warn the students about the possibility of having this kind of interviewee.

- **Activity #4: (10 minutes) Creating the protocol**
  Students will use the final 10 minutes of the class to create a protocol for the interview, in which they state who they are, why are they doing the interview, ask for permission to record and select between 6 and 8 important questions to ask.

Resources for teachers:

- Journalism, Good Questions to Ask a Reporter: http://tiny.cc/G7L3R1
- Sample Interview Protocol: http://tiny.cc/G7L3R2
- Semi Structured Interview Protocol: http://tiny.cc/G7L3R3
- How to Conduct a Journalistic Interview: http://tiny.cc/G7L3R4

Grade 7 Lesson 4

"What Makes a Change Maker? Learning from Leaders of Change"

Time Frame: 60 Min. | **Subject Area:** Social Studies, Civics, Reading and/or Language Arts
Designer: Tatiana Shevchenko

Standards: Reduced Inequality (SDG 10), Industry, Innovation and Infrastructure (SDG 9), Quality Education (SDG 4), Gender Equality (SDG 5), however lesson can be applicable to all 17 Sustainable Development Goals, depending on the issues the students see in their community contexts.

Summary and Rationale: This lesson aims to help students better understand the characteristics of change makers by reviewing their findings after having conducted interviews with change makers.

Instructional goals: Students will use higher level analytical thinking to understand the character traits of change agents and to compare and contrast them with their own character traits, thus understanding that they too can become change agents. Students will use sketchnoting as a visual means to depict, organize and analyze information from interviews. Students will build a class venn diagram to make comparisons and make connections among their interviewees and each other in order to better understand and communicate what they learned after conducting interviews.

Understanding: After conducting interviews with change makers, students will share their findings with the class. Students will learn about the different types of change makers, their personality traits and biographical information. Students will analyze what it takes to become a changemaker and will examine what impact one person can have on the lives of others. Likewise, students will understand that they too can become change makers.

Essential Questions:
* Who are the people who create change? (biographical information)
* What are the character traits of these people? How are they similar and different?
* What inspires people to take action?

173

- What are the types of actions a change maker can take?
- How does the scope of action differ?
- What are the challenges that these people face?
- How can the actions of an individual have a broader impact on their communities or the world?
- What and how can we learn by studying the lives of others?
- How can we become change makers ourselves?

Student Learning Objectives (Students Will be Able To): Students will develop an understanding of what it takes to be a changemaker and how changemaker character traits might be similar or different from their own. Students will understand that they too can become change makers.

Students will be able to:

- Speak clearly and succinctly describing their findings from interviews with change makers.
- Use the sketchnote technique to organize and analyze their learnings and to combine them with others.
- Listen to their peers and look for similarities and differences in findings.
- Work on small and large teams to achieve a common task.
- Develop creative ways to depict and share a lot of information in a condensed and succinct way.

Assessments:

Students will be assessed based on their participation in the storytelling, organizing information on the Sketchnote poster, presenting, and partaking in the class venn diagram activity. Active participation will require students to share their ideas, listen to the ideas of others, and contribute to the class discussion.

Sequence of Activities:

- **5 minutes - Introduction :**
  The instructor splits students into groups of 3. Students have conducted interviews with change makers and are ready to present their findings. Students are given instructions to present their interviews to each other within their small groups. As they present they are instructed to compare and contrast their change makers.

174

Students work as a group to depict their findings on a poster using Sketchnotes. Students are then told that after the small groups have completed their presentations to each other, the class will work together to create a changemaker venn diagram where the class will analyze how the characteristics of change makers compare to the characteristics of seventh grade students.

- **20 minutes - Sharing and Sketchnotes:**
  In groups of 3 students work to present their interviewee
  Students are tasked with creating a sketchnote poster to depict their change agents' experiences. Once groups complete their posters they put them up around the classroom.

- **10 minutes - Poster presentation**
  Each team (3 people per team based on class of 30 people) take 1 minute to presents their poster highlighting the main takeaways from their group discussion.

- **20 minutes - Class Venn Diagram**
  Students work together to create a large class venn diagram which depicts (by comparing and contrasting) the characteristics of the change agents interviewed by students and the characteristics of students in their class.

**Examples of items which might be included in the changemaker venn diagram

Change makers:
- o   Are the first to take action
- o   Sometimes have to overcome adversity
- o   Experience resistance initially
- o   Develop their ideas
- o   Rally people around their beliefs
- o   Hold firm beliefs

Examples of items which might be included in the **overlap** part of the diagram:
- o   Are energetic
- o   Are optimistic
- o   Are ambitious
- o   Are a part of a community

- ○ Have families
- ○ Have dreams
- ○ Have the ability to learn new things and organize ideas

Examples of items which might be included in the **7th graders** side of the diagram:
- ○ Are dependent on their parents
- ○ Don't always have the right resources (money, time)
- ○ Cannot easily have influence over adults who often make decisions

- **5 minutes - Concluding remarks**
  The instructor points out that change agents and their causes might seem all very different, but that they have many overlapping characteristics with each other, as well as with the 7th grade class. The instructor also points out that the characteristics of the class which are different from change agents are those that likely can be learned and developed. The instructor asks students to reflect on this before next class.

Resources for Students:
- *Resources for students are context dependent and assume access to internet and understanding of the English Language
- Students will need pens and poster paper, additional stationary material could be provided (glue, scissors, magazines for picture cut-outs, glitter, ribbons etc)
- If students used video recording devices (cameras, phones, computers) to collect and share interview, those devices need to be available in class.

Resources for Teachers:
- Change Makers Lesson Plan: http://tiny.cc/G7L4R1
- Venn Diagram Templates: http://tiny.cc/G7L4R2
- Sketchnote Strategies: http://tiny.cc/G7L4R3
- Sketchnotes: http://tiny.cc/G7L4R4

Grade 7 Lesson 5

"Looking Toward Future Change"

Time Frame: 60 minutes | **Subjects:** Social Studies, Science |
Designer: Katherine Kinnaird

Standards: Reduced Inequalities (SDG 10), Peace, Justice, and Strong Institutions (SDG 16), Partnerships for the Goals (SDG 17)

Summary and Rationale: Based on the interviews they have completed and their class presentations, students will explore ways that they themselves can become changemakers in their communities and the world. At this crucial point in their education, they will learn how to apply the skills they have already developed to their future studies and lives.

Instructional Goals: Students will learn how to identify an important social issue and work with other students to construct a systematic plan to resolve that issue in the future. In social studies, they will develop an understanding of social justice issues. In science, they will use the scientific method to define a problem, do research about it, hypothesize a solution, test their solution, analyze the results, refine the solution, and share an action plan with the class.

Understanding Goals: Students will understand the importance of working together to create change. They will develop collaboration, research, analytical, and communication skills. In the process, they will experience the challenges and rewards that accompany the work of social reform.

Essential Questions:
- What issues does my community face?
- What issues does the world face? Are they the same as those in my community?
- How are all of these social issues connected with one another?
- Which of my classmates researched each issue? With whom can I work to create change?

Student Learning Objectives (Students Will be Able To):
- Work and communicate effectively with their classmates

- Express their ideas about important social issues
- Think critically about how to resolve social issues
- Creatively and scientifically develop social action plans

Assessment: The teacher can grade students' action plans and class presentations using the International Baccalaureate (IB) system's Approaches to Learning (ATL) <u>framework</u> for the Middle Years Program (MYP).

- *Novice/Beginning (N)* - Students are beginning to understand the research and collaboration process, but do not take an active role in developing a social action plan.
- *Learner/Developing (L)* - Students work with others and participate in creating a social action plan with constant guidance from the teacher.
- *Practitioner/Using (P)* - Students work well in their groups and confidently present their group's social action plan to the rest of the class.
- *Expert/Sharing (E)* - Students are leaders in their groups and help struggling students. They confidently share their social action plan *and* its future significance with the class.

Sequence of Activities:

- **Opening Activity:** Students brainstorm all of the social issues that they researched in their interviews. They make one list about the issues facing their community and another about the issues facing the world. Students identify where the issues facing their community and the world overlap.

  Based on their analysis of the key issues, students divide themselves into groups to address one problem. Note: it is important that students divide themselves into groups rather than the teacher because they need to learn to make analytical connections between their interview research topics and their classmates' topics. Once students divide themselves, the teacher can verify their groups and make any necessary adjustments.

- **Main Activity:** As a group, students use the scientific method to define the problem they are going to address, share their thoughts about the problem based on their interview research, hypothesize a solution to the problem, brainstorm the problems and successes that might emerge with that solution, refine their solution, and develop an action plan.

- **Closing Activity:** Students share their thought process and final action plan with the class.

Resources for Students:
- Steps of the Scientific Method: http://tiny.cc/G7L5R1

Resources for Teachers:
- Global Issues: http://tiny.cc/G7L5R2

Grade 8

Lesson Overview
Learning Goal
In Grade 8, students will explore the theme of injustice: what it means, how it manifests in everyday life, and how it contributes to larger social dynamics. Students will also evaluate our shared values, discuss why it is important to ensure equality among all people, and brainstorm ways to promote equality and justice in their own lives

Lesson Scaffold	
Lesson 1	**What is Injustice to Me?**
Lesson 2	**What is Injustice to Other People?**
Lesson 3	**What are our Shared Values and Why Should Everyone Be Treated Equally?**
Lesson 4	**What Can We Do?**
Lesson 5	**Take Action!**

Learning Objectives
<ul><li>Students will understand the causes and effects of global injustice and inequality.</li><li>Students will become cognizant of the effects of these forces in their own lives.</li><li>Students will become empowered to promote equality and justice in their everyday lives</li></ul>

Grade 8 Lesson 1

"What is Injustice to Me?"

Time Frame: 40 minutes | **Subjects:** Civic, social studies, history | **Designer:** Maria Lee

Standards: Peace, Justice, Strong Institutions (SDG 16)

Summary & Rationale: Students will be asked to think about the times they each personally faced "injustice." They will be encouraged to reflect on what had happened, why they thought the situation was unjust, and how they felt throughout the entire experience. We would eventually like students to be able to understand what injustice means, to identify moments when others are facing injustice, and to act on it as social agents. However, in order to be able to progress through these stages, each student will first need to identify and experience injustice first-hand so they can have an easier time relating to others facing injustice.

Instructional Goal: To encourage students to identify and to reflect on times they personally experienced injustice -- intrapersonal skills: introspective reflection

Understanding Goals: What is injustice to me? How do I define injustice? How do I feel when unjust incidents happen to me?

Essential Questions: What is injustice? How did/does injustice affect me?

Student Learning Objectives (Students Will be Able To):
- Identify moments they experienced certain emotions
- Describe and categorize those emotions
- Translate those feelings into words
- Reflect on why they experienced those emotions.

Assessment: Informal checks for understanding: teachers will be able to probe and ask questions: "how did you react to it?" "how did you feel?" "why do you think you felt that way?"

Sequence of Activities:

- Teacher hands out a post-it to each student and asks him/her to write a definition for "injustice"
- Teacher collects the post-it notes and puts it in a bag
- Teacher facilitates discussion on: "did you ever experience injustice?"
- Teacher intentionally doesn't give any examples so that the teacher's definition/example of injustice will not affect students' answers
- While facilitating, teacher makes sure that the student who shares addresses: what happened, why it was unjust, how they felt, how they reacted to it
- When it is almost time to finish, teacher pulls out the bag with definitions and gives it to the students. The bag will go around so that each student can pull one out and read aloud the one they pick.
- Ask open-ended questions about the definitions that come up: what do you think about these definitions? How would you define injustice? Do you want to add anything?
- As a class, students and teacher come up with one concrete definition of "injustice"

Resources for Teachers:

Ten Strategies for Effective Discussion Leading: http://tiny.cc/G8L1R1

Grade 8 Lesson 2

"What is Injustice to Other People?"

Time Frame: 40 minutes | **Subjects:** Civics, social studies, history | **Designer:** Maria Lee

Standards: Peace, Justice, Strong Institutions (SDG 16), Reduced Inequalities (SDG 10)

Summary & Rationale: Now that students have been able to identify moments of injustice in their personal lives, it will be necessary to develop the ability to recognize injustice happening in their surrounding environment, whether it is in the local community or global context. Students must be able to view injustice from another person's perspective in order to realize that they themselves must become social agents fighting for justice on other people's behalf.

Instructional Goal: To be able to place themselves in another person's position to recognize and to acknowledge instances of injustice occurring in their context

Understanding Goals: What is injustice? How does everyone define injustice? What does injustice look like?

Essential Questions: How do other people interpret injustice? Where is injustice happening right now?

Student Learning Objectives (Students Will be Able To):
- Identify instances where people experience injustice.
- Examine and assess whether someone is experiencing injustice in a given situation.

Assessment: Informal checks of understanding: teacher will facilitate group discussion. Additionally, since not all students will have the chance to share their experiences, they will be asked to write about it (while reflecting upon the discussion questions from today's class) in a free-writing style for homework.

Sequence of Activities:

- Review definition of "justice" that the students developed in Lesson #1
- Keeping that in mind, teacher presents students with a photo of a group of people getting ready to compete in a race (see photo in the resources section below).
- After students analyze the photo for a while, students are put into pairs to share their thoughts. No specific questions are asked by the teacher.
- The class comes back together and teacher facilitates discussion touching upon:
  - What is this picture about?
  - What is happening in the picture?
  - Who are the participants in the race?
  - What does the referee say?
  - Why does the referee say this?
  - How or how isn't he saying the "correct" phrase?
  - Is this race truly "fair?"
  - What makes a race fair?
  - Why is/isn't it fair? (teacher plays devil's advocate)
  - Touch upon the topic of:
    - Different perspectives/circumstances
    - How we can interpret things differently from a different perspective
- Place discussion within a bigger context:
  - Were there ever instances of injustice taking place in our surroundings (not directly to us, though)?
  - Did you notice it? Can you even think of a particular instance?
  - Did other people near you not notice it?
  - Were there times when you didn't notice it, but other people did?
  - Why do you think there are such differences between people?

Resources for Teachers:

Image to start discussion

Grade 8 Lesson 3

**"What is Human Dignity?
What are our Shared Values and Why Should Everyone be Treated Equally?"**

Time Frame: 40 minutes | **Subjects:** Civic, social studies, language and communication
Designer: Wendi Cui

Standards: Peace, Justice, Strong Institutions (SDG 16)

Instructional Goal: Students will build the shared value of humanity

Summary & Rationale: The current lesson is in a sequence of five lessons on peace and social justice. In this lesson, students will explore the concepts of human dignity, social dilemma, etc., and understand the nature of humanitarian acts. Lastly they will reflect on what they can do as bystanders.

Understanding Goal: social rules, human dignity, dilemma, social pressure, role of bystanders, humanitarian acts.

Essential Questions: What is human dignity? What can we do to protect human dignity? What are the risks?

Student Learning Objectives (Students Will be Able To):
- Understand the meaning of human dignity
- Identify a social dilemma and tell the difference between the roles in the dilemma
- Explain the reason and risks in conducting humanitarian acts
- Reflect on their own role in everyday life.

Assessment: The teacher can ask the following questions to check students' understanding: "Can you give an example of the violation of human dignity?" "What is the dilemma in this example?" "What is your role in this situation, can you act?"

Sequence of Activities:

- (5 minutes) Warm up: students discuss in pairs to define concepts of "human dignity", "social dilemma", and "bystanders", then share their views with class. See definitions below.
- (8 minutes) Class reading: teachers can use the story of "Brave Shopkeeper" listed in the resource section below, but they are also encouraged to find a story in the national/local context.
- (10 minutes) Group discussion on reading guided questions.
- (10 minutes) Class discussion on guiding questions and teacher presentation of key concepts.
- (7 minutes) Reflection on real life examples.

Resources for Teachers:
- Center for Civic Education, Examining Conflict Resolution: http://tiny.cc/G8L3R1
- RCRC Humanitarian education: http://tiny.cc/G8L3R2
- Red Cross Lesson Plan on Humanitarian Education: http://tiny.cc/G8L3R3
- Humanitarian Learning Portal: http://tiny.cc/G8L3R4
- World's Largest Lesson: http://tiny.cc/G8L3R5

Key definitions:
- **Human dignity:** (self) respect.
- **A bystander** is someone who is aware of an incident, without being involved, where the life or human dignity of others is in danger. The bystander has to decide whether to act or not, because doing either may put him or her − or the people he or she is trying to protect − at risk, physically or materially. Either choice can have complex and long-term consequences for all involved.
- **Social pressure** is the influence exerted by family, friends or other groups of people that puts pressure on an individual to behave in a particular manner.
- **A dilemma** is a situation that requires a choice between options that are or seem equally unfavourable or mutually exclusive.
- **A humanitarian** act is an act carried out to protect someone whose life or human dignity is in danger, especially someone whom one would not ordinarily be inclined to help or protect. Such acts are likely to involve personal or material risk

---

Grade 8 Lesson 4

"What Can We Do?"

Time Frame: 40 minutes | **Subjects**: social studies, language courses | **Designer**: Xin Miao

Standards: Peace, Justice, and Strong Institutions (SDG 16)

Summary and Rationale: In this class, students are expected to identify one situation where they have encountered injustices or see injustices happened to other people, and analyze that situation.

Instructional Goal: Students are expected to develop the awareness to recognize differences, respect shared values, empathetically approach human interaction, and actively seek solutions to address injustices. Discover one unjust situation in their personal life, in school, in the community or from news reports.

Understanding Goal: Justice is a complex topic which may appear to be subjective and may heavily depend on the perspective of the parties involved. It is complex, yet plausible to address and resolve some unjust situations.

Essential questions:
- What is injustice to me?
- What is injustice to others?
- In a shared world we live in, what are the shared values?
- What causes injustice? Who are the major parties involved in unjust situations?
- Who is responsible to correct an injustice? What is the relevance of your perspective to how you perceive an injustice (does it depend which side of the injustice you're on)?
- Would you address injustices if they happen to you? How would you do? In what way?

Student Learning Objectives (Students Will be Able To):
- Engage in teamwork.
- Apply and analyze logically. Apply knowledge from previous 3 classes and personal experience to solidify the concept of justice, differences,

peace and shared values such as empathy and respect. And develop analyzing skills to identify parties involved in an unjust situation and dig into causes of an unjust situation.
- Communication, oral presentation skills

Assessment:
- Student self-assessment - students will reflect on how well they engaged with their peers and how well they presented their ideas to the class.
- Teacher evaluation - written feedback and comments on students' self assessment.

Sequence of Activities:

- Warm-up: Invite students to share injustices that they have experienced.
- Input: present photos or videos of injustices in different situations (e.g., bully or specific court cases that are region and country specific.
- Form Groups: Identify and analyze one unjust situation. Describe ways in which it could be made just.
- Group Presentation: Students present to the class how they sought out to correct injustices in their respective groups. As a class students discuss the solutions proposed by groups focusing on the definition of justice and perspective. Striving to answer the question does perspective matter? Whose perspective matters? Why does perspective matter and how does it relate to justice, if at all?

Resources for teachers:
- Book - *Justice* by Michael J. Sandel

Grade 8 Lesson 5

"Take Action! Creatively seek solutions to Address Unjust Situations"

Time Frame: 60 minutes | **Subjects**: social studies, language courses | **Designer**: Xin Miao
Standards: SDG 16 Peace, Justice, and Institution

Summary and Rationale: In this class, students are expected to build on the previous session, they refresh their memory on the injustices presented in the previous class and strive to outline a list of challenges they encountered when proposing solutions. As a class students pick one injustice they want to address and prepare a detailed plan on how to address this injustice.

Instructional Goal: Students are expected to seek solutions to the one situation they agreed upon as unjust. Students learn to develop action plans to address injustices.

Understanding Goals: Students will understand that they have the power to affect change in real-life situations of injustice by working collaboratively and exploring examples of change agents who addressed injustices (in U.S. Context, ex. Rosa Parks, the Suffragettes - women's voting rights movement, the 2017 Women's March).

Essential questions:
- Who are the people who address injustices?
- How do people address injustices?
- What can an individual do to undress injustice?
- Does everyone in a community always agree on what is just and unjust?
- When tackling an unjust issue what are the steps a group must take?
- What would different institutions do to address injustices, such as social media, law enforcement body, government, etc?
- What is the difference between grassroots and political efforts?

Student Learning Objectives (Students Will be Able To):
- Team work

193

- Analyzing and negotiation skills
- Communication, oral presentation skills
- Creatively formulate solutions.
- Researching and analysing social justice movement
- Synthesizing research and formulating a strategy

Assessment:
- Students write a reflection on how they understand injustice and how they believe this compares to the way they communicated their ideas during class.
- Teacher evaluation is a set of comments and feedback to the students' reflections.

Sequence of Activities:
- 10 Minutes - the teacher introduces several social justice movements that are context specific or globally recognized, the teacher asks students to look for commonalities or differences in the movements.
- 5 Minutes - Students are asked to reflect on the previous class and the topics they presented in small teams. Students vote on a topic to discuss in class. (Ex. oil spill)
- 25 Minutes - Students discuss the topic of injustice and brainstorm possible solutions. Students think about the stakeholders that the injustice effects and map (on the board) the respective perspectives of the stakeholders (ex. Animals, oil companies, citizens of the community where the oil spill happened, government etc.). Ex. pros and cons of the injustice, and the solution to the injustice.
- 15 Minutes - Students deliberate on a solution that would address the interests of most stakeholders connected with the injustice. Students plan and present their solution.
- 5 Minutes - Closing remarks and reflections.

Grade 9

Lesson Overview	
Learning Goal	
In Grade 9, students will examine topics related to women's rights and gender equality through literature. Using these literary portrayals of women, students will explore gender inequality as it exists at the local, national, and global levels. Finally, students will design, implement and present a project based on what they have learned.	
Lesson Scaffold	
Lesson 1	**Looking towards Literature: How are women portrayed in a global context?**
Lesson 2	**Analyzing Literature: How are women are portrayed in their community?**
Lesson 3	**Learning from Literature: Current reality of women in the community**
Lesson 4	**Designing a Project to Address Gender Inequalities**
Lesson 5	**Implementing a Project**
Learning Objectives	
<ul><li>Students will practice critical reading as they explore social issues through literature.</li><li>Students will draw lessons from works of literature and apply take-aways to their own lives.</li><li>Students will design and implement an independent project on what they have learned.</li></ul>	

Grade 9 Lesson 1

"Women's Rights Movements: Positioning/Dive Into Literature"

Time Frame: 60 minutes | **Subjects**: History, Social Sciences, Civics | **Designer**: Matt Owens

Standards: SDG 5 (Gender Equality and the Empowerment of Women and Girls), 10 (Reduce Inequalities), 16 (Peace, Justice, and Strong Institutions)

Summary and Rationale:
To provide a social and historical framework as a foundation for the following lessons in which students examine gender inequality and women's rights movements through short stories and poems

Instructional Goals:
- Students will gain a greater appreciation of women's rights movements throughout history, forming a context through which the literature in the next lessons can be read
- Students will form a foundation that will allow them to read their short story or poem with a critical eye

Understanding Goals:
- Women's rights movements have a strong and vibrant history and presence in international society today.
- Women's rights movements from all over the world have worked tirelessly to address the inequalities that have existed in societies throughout history and still exist today.

Essential questions:
- What inequalities have women encountered throughout history and today?
- How have women and women's rights movements responded to inequalities throughout history?
- What major social and historical forces have shaped the rise of women's rights movements?
- How might literature serve as an appropriate lens through which women's rights can be examined?

Student Learning Objectives (Students Will be Able To):
- Students will be able to engage in a meaningful discussion about the role of women's rights movements have played in addressing gender inequalities.
- Students will be able to form a critical framework to forge connections with the literature they will read in subsequent classes

Assessment: Class Discussion

Sequence of Activities:

- *Introduction (10 minutes)*
  The instructor provides a brief introduction to women's rights movements throughout history and in the present, taking care to include movements from across the world.

- *Primary Source Readings (20 minutes)*
  The instructor divides students into small groups and distributes primary source documents. Students spend the first 10 minutes reading their piece silently. They then discuss in small groups the questions prompted by the instructor. What inequalities or tensions do students notice? How might they be addressed?

- *Class Discussion (20 minutes)*
  Students reconvene as a class to discuss the their different pieces, common themes, and differences across cultures. The instructor may also choose to rearrange groups so that students can discuss their piece with students who read different pieces.

- *Literature (10 minutes)*
  Teacher presents the different texts that students may read for their literature analysis. Students choose the text they will read for the following class

Resources for Students
Primary Sources for Women's History: http://tiny.cc/G9L1R1
Resources for teachers:
History of International Women's Movements
- Key Dates in International Women's History: http://tiny.cc/G9L1R2
- UN Women: http://tiny.cc/G9L1R3

Grade 9 Lesson 2

"Literature Analysis - How Women are Portrayed in their Community"

Time Frame: 50 minutes | **Subjects**: Literature/Social Studies |
Designer: Cassie Fuenmayor
Standards: SDG 5 (Gender Equality and the Empowerment of Women and Girls)

Summary and Rationale: This lesson will center around an analysis of the literature that students chose in lesson one. They will analyze (in groups) the ways that women are represented within the Literature, and what aspects of the literature form/contribute to this representation.

Instructional Goals:
- Students will cultivate an appreciation, curiosity, and respect for cultural diversity
- Students will practice critical thinking and analysis skills when looking at poetry/novels/short stories

Competencies:
- Cultivate an appreciation, curiosity, and respect for cultural diversity and world culture as the foundation for self-reflection, identity formation, and empathetically approaching human interaction.
- Establish a solid foundation in world history, geography and culture, as well as explore world literature
- Question the existing power structures and be aware of their place within a specific world context
- Understand one's own identity and roots, others' identities and roots, how cultures shape identities, and where one is situated in space and time (Self-Awareness)
- Recognize cultural prejudice and the ability to minimize its effect
- Understand how values are created through culture, religion, and experience

Understanding Goals:
- Students will begin to understand the ways that Literature can both accurately and inaccurately represent social and cultural realities.

Essential questions:
- How are women represented in the Literature you read?
- How does this fit into the context/setting of the Literature or the author?
- What does this representation of women show us about different cultures
- Do we see any inequalities or imbalances of power in this literature?

Student Learning Objectives (Students Will be Able To):
- Students will end the lesson with an understanding of how women are represented in the context of the literature they read.
- Students will begin to think about the ways that the literature accurately and inaccurately reflected cultural realities

Assessment: Teacher can circulate and monitor group discussions

Sequence of Activities:

- **(25 min) Students will meet in small groups to discuss their chosen piece of Literature:**
  Discussion Questions:
  - What do you know about the setting/context/author of the literature you read?
  - How are women represented in the Literature you read?
  - How does this fit into the context/setting of the Literature or the author?
  - What does this representation of women show us about different cultures
  - Do we see any inequalities or imbalances of power in this literature?
  - Do you think this representation is accurate for the context?

- **(25 min) Students will meet in different groups to share about the literature they read with a group who didn't read it, once everyone shares, students will answer discussion questions**
  Discussion Questions:
  - Do you see any similarities/differences between the way women are represented?
  - In which context are women portrayed positively? Negatively?

Grade 9 Lesson 3

"Making Connections from Literature to Current Realities: Women in Our Community"

Timeframe: 50-60 minutes | **Subjects**: Literature, Social Studies | **Designer**: Heather Kesselman

Standards: SDG 5 (Gender, Equality and the Empowerment of Women and Girls), SDG 10 (Reduced Inequalities), SDG 16 (Peace, Justice and Strong Institutions)

Summary and Rationale: Students will make connections between the themes of female empowerment in the literature and the role of women in their own lives and society. This is important in personalizing notions of gender equality in a specific context.

Instructional Goal: Students will make connections to the current realities in their own communities.

Understanding Goals:
- Literature can imitate life and reflect social inequalities in our own world
- The role of women in society is complex and fundamentally unequal

Essential questions:
- How are the ways women are represented in literature visible or invisible in your own society?
- How are women treated unfairly in your society?
- What are the underlying power structures and cultural values that define the treatment of women in your society?

Student Learning Objectives (Students Will be Able To):
- Students will be able to analyze gender inequalities in their communities
- Students will be able to describe comparisons and differences to the role of women in the literature.

Assessment: Mini-poster, Final reflection

Sequence of Activities:

- **Freewriting (5 minutes):** Students describe in writing a prominent woman in their life or community. What power does she have? What struggles does she face? What social or cultural expectations restrain her or empower her? What choices can she make and what choices are made for her? How would her life or opportunities be different if she were male?
- **Pair Share (5 minutes):** Students share the story of the woman they described with a partner, discussing the question "How does her gender influence her opportunities, choices, attitudes or goals?"
- **Whole Group Share (5 minutes):** 2-3 Students share what they discussed with their partners.
- **Connection to Literature:**
  - **Literature Analysis (20 minutes):** In partners, students collect examples of at least 5 quotes or anecdotes from the literature that speaks to the treatment of women in the story, and record these notes with some inferences/analysis next to each example. This can be done in two-column Cornell Notes, a graphic organizer of the teacher's choosing, or an organized table in students' notebooks.
  - **Share Findings (3 minutes):** Students share whole-group some of the examples they found, comparing common findings and differences. This should help struggling students fill in any gaps in their analysis.
  - **Create a Visual (10 minutes)**
    - Students create a Venn Diagram or other infographic of choice comparing the role of women in the literature and that of women in their own society.
  - **Presentation - Gallery Walk (3 minutes)**
    - Students walk around the room and observe the common themes identified by classmates.
- **Final Reflection (8 minutes)**
  - Students respond in their notebook: What similarities and differences can we observe between the role of women in the literature and in our own society?

Resources for teachers:
- Venn Diagram Worksheet: http://tiny.cc/G9L3R1

Grade 9 Lesson 4

"Designing a Project to Address Gender Inequalities"

Time Frame: 50 - 120 minutes | **Subjects**: Literature, Social Studies
Designer: Christian Bautista
Standards: SDG 5 (Gender, Equality and the Empowerment of Women and Girls), SDG 10 (Reduced Inequalities), SDG 16 (Peace, Justice and Strong Institutions)

Summary and Rationale: Design a work of art that addresses any gender inequalities in student's own communities; this work can be a short story, poem, painting, drawing, sculpture, song, composition, etc. as appropriate or desired by the teacher or students. This lesson could be planned in collaboration with an elective fine or performing art teacher.

Instructional Goal: Students will apply their creativity to a social issue in their own life and/or community in a way that synthesizes their work in previous lessons and engages stakeholders beyond the walls of the classroom.

Understanding Goals (Big Ideas):
- Fine and performing arts as expressive media can serve as a jumping off point for social movements
- Authentic social and political issues can be addressed even by young students when they act with honesty, solidarity, and creativity

Essential questions:
- How might art represent the inequities explored in previous lessons?
- Are artistic media uniquely useful in the pursuit of social justice?
- What are the limits of each particular medium (painting, singing, etc.) to achieve social justice? What are the strengths?
- How can art shape culture and society?

Student Learning Objectives (Students Will be Able To):
- Students will create an original work of art that reflects their personal learning in lessons 1-3
- Students will explain through written or verbal reflection why they made the artistic decisions they made

Assessment: Presentation of Produced Art Product, Written or Verbal Reflection

Sequence of Activities:
- **Connection to Literature, Freewriting (5-7 minutes):** Students freewrite about any developments in their thinking over the course of the first 2 lessons. They should review the 5 quotes that they collected from lesson 3 as well as any quotes from their classmates that they found interesting; they should reflect upon the relevance of these quotes to their own lives and in their own communities.
- **Production of Art Deliverable (20-60 minutes):** Students should use the majority of the allotted time to develop their work of art that attempt to wrestle with one or more of these essential questions:
  - What inequalities have women, particularly in our community, encountered throughout history and today?
  - How has our community (My school? My city? My state? My country?) responded to inequalities throughout history?
  - Is there a way to portray artistically the major social and historical forces have shaped the rise of women's rights movements?
- If students are producing a painting, collage, or other work of visual art, it is suggested that the teacher limit students to a predetermined artistic medium according to availability or opportunity to collaborate with another instructor (music instructor, art instructor, etc.).
  - **Suggested Media:**
    - A collage with photos from the students' own life or from local newspapers, websites, etc. Any form of painting, perhaps with some formal limitation (use only 2 colors, etc.)
    - Photography, Poetry, Narrative Writing, Songwriting or Lyrics

- **Final Reflection (20 minutes)**
  Depending on the nature of the deliverable, students should either spend time writing a response to one of the 3 essential questions above or verbally presenting their work to the class at large. If projects are sufficiently large (or have taken more than a single class to produce) the teacher should consider holding a separate event to which community members (teachers, administrators, and parents) will be invited to view the students' work.

Grade 9 Lesson 5

"Implementing a Project"

Time Frame: 120-180 minutes | **Subjects:** Literature, Art, Social Studies, Community Engagement | **Designer:** Chihiro Yoshida

Standards: SDG 5 (Gender, Equality and the Empowerment of Women and Girls), SDG 10 (Reduced Inequalities), SDG 16 (Peace, Justice and Strong Institutions)

Summary and Rationale: Using the artwork that they had created in Lesson 4 as a medium, students will share it with a wider community in a public space and lead a discussion on topics of gender inequality that may be taking place within the community.

Instructional Goal: Students will present and share their artwork with the wider community, practice public speaking, and learn to engage other community members in a discussion on social issues.

Understanding Goals: Big ideas (building on Lesson 4)
- Fine and performing arts as expressive media can serve as a jumping off point for social movements
- Authentic social and political issues can be addressed even by young students when they act with honesty, solidarity, and creativity
- Engaging in conversations with community members can be a driving force for action

Essential questions:
- How can youth challenge pre-existing notions of social and gender inequality?
- How can art be used as a medium to inspire and engage a wider community to participate in discussions on social issues?
- Who are the stakeholders within the local community that should be involved in conversations in order to instigate wider action?

Student Learning Objectives (Students Will be Able To):
- Students will practice and learn to speak in front of large audiences

- Students will learn to lead a conversation with different stakeholders on gender issues

Sequence of Activities:
- **Brainstorming (60 minutes):** Students work in pairs or small groups to reflect back on the artwork they produced and discuss how to most effectively present and share the artwork with community members. They may choose to;
    - Add a descriptive written statement to explain their artwork.
    - Perform a short art piece showing the work
    - Explain their artwork to visitors who go around the booths

- **Presentation (20 minutes):** The artwork will be shared in a public event, organized at a public library, community organization, church, park, etc, that can attract many community members to visit and engage with the students. The school and teachers will work with local institutions to organize the event, and students will present their artwork to visitors.

- **Discussion (40 minutes):** Students and community members then break up into small discussion groups to engage in conversations (led by students) about the artwork and gender inequality issues that they attempt to address. Some guiding questions are;
    - What emotions did the artwork evoke in you?
    - Do you agree/disagree with the messages of the artwork? How might some voices be left out of the discussion?
    - How can the community do better to address such gender issues?
    - What do you think your role in this endeavor can be?

- **Reflection (15 minutes/later day):** Student come back to the classroom to engage in a discussion to share their discussions with community members, and how they can take the initiatives forward. They may also engage in individual reflection through writing in journals.

Resources for teachers:
- UN Women - Youth Powering Gender Equality: http://tiny.cc/G9L5R1
- A guide to Empower Young People to Become Advocates for Gender Equality: http://tiny.cc/G9L5R2
- Civic Engagement in Diverse Contexts: http://tiny.cc/G9L5R3

Grade 10

Lesson Overview

Learning Goal

Grade 10's curriculum is focused on the student's individual sense of agency. Over the course of five lessons, students will identify their own values, explore how they express those values through their actions, and go out into their communities to see how they can contribute to solving real-world problems

Lesson Scaffold	
Lesson 1	My Self
Lesson 2	My Community
Lesson 3	Balancing Voices in Global Issues
Lesson 4	Our World
Lesson 5	Capstone Project

Learning Objectives

- Students will think critically about how values relate to actions, and practice how they can promote their values in common scenarios.
- Students will engage with a real-world problem in their own community, talking to people and developing their own solution.
- Students will practice formal writing in their final paper.

Grade 10 Lesson 1

"Self"

Time Frame: 60 mins | **Subjects:** Arts |
Designer: Sharon Jiae Lee
Standards: SDG 1 (End Poverty), 2 (Zero Hunger), 3 (Good Health and Well-Being), 4 (Quality Education), 5 (Gender Equality), 10 (Reduced Inequalities), 16 (Peace, Justice and Strong Institutions), 17 (Partnerships for the Goals)

Summary and Rationale: In this lesson, students will draw their values and share them with the classroom and identify situations/places/events in the community and the world where those values are being lived out and are lacking. For instance, a student may value family support the most and through discussions, realize that the places family support is lacking the most are orphanages. In the following lessons, students will turn towards the community, the nation, and the world to find solutions to the problems they have identified and finally write a paper stating the problem and offering solutions to the problems they feel most passionate to solve. (*Note: materials for the lesson are always adjustable to the context of the classroom.)

Instructional Goals:
- Students will be able to know themselves better by reflecting on the values that they have.
- Students will learn to have constructive discussions about the different values of other classmates and learn to respect those differences.
- Students will be able to identify gaps/problems in their community, country, and or world where those values are lacking.

Understanding Goals:
- People hold different values and they act on those values to make everyday decisions.
- Dissimilar values should be respected and if some seem incompatible, students should be able to have constructive dialogues to understand and resolve conflicts.

Essential questions:
- What are values?
- What are your most important values in life?
- Why should we care about values?
- Where in our community, nation, and or world do we see our values lived out and where do we not see our values lived out?

Student Learning Objectives (Students Will be Able To): with Assessment Checklist:

Objective	Conditions	Observable Skill/Behavior	Assessment
Learning what values are and why they are important	In class as a whole	Students will understand what values are and why they are important	Can the student explain what values are and why they are important in life?
Reflecting and identifying personal values	Individual work	Students will identify one important value in their lives	Can the student identify one important value in his/her life?
Cooperating with other students in their groups	Group work	Students will share their own values, listen to the values of others, and provide constructive feedback and ask helpful questions.	Can the student work together in groups? Does the student respect different values of other students? Does the student provide constructive feedback and/or ask helpful questions?
Connecting their personal values to the world	Group work	Students will identify problems in their community/nation/world that go against their values.	Can the student make connections between his/her personal values and the community/nation/world and make connections?

210

Sequence of activities:

Time spent on activity	Activity	Questions
Opening (20 mins)	-Hand out a piece of paper to each student. (*Note: materials for the lesson are always adjustable to the context of the classroom.) -Open the lesson by asking the questions on the right column to the students. -After having several students answer the questions, ask them to reflect on their own values and draw one value on the piece of paper. They should draw a scene/event/object that *best* represents that value. For instance, if a student values friendship, he/she might draw something fun that he/she did with friends.	*What are values? Why are they important?*
Presentation & Group Discussion (20 mins)	-Have students split up into different groups (small enough where students have time to share their values to each other). -Ask students to guess each other's values. For instance, students might see a drawing of friends having fun and say, "I think you value *friendship.*" Have students share their values. -After students share their values within their groups, ask the questions on the right column. Have students discuss the questions within their groups.	*Do you think everyone has the same values? Why or why not? Is it okay to have different values? Should all values be treated equal? What if some values are contradictory? What should we do in that case?*
Group Discussion (15 mins)	-Ask the students about values in the community/nation/world. Ask the questions on the right column. Have students discuss in their groups.	*Where in our community do you see your value lived out? Where in the country do*

		you see your value lived out? Where in the world do you see your value lived out? *On the contrary, where do you not see it lived out?*
Closing (5 mins)	-Have some volunteers present their drawings and their values to the whole class. Ask "What do should we do when we see problems in the world that go against what we think is important in life?" Encourage students to be change-makers in their communities and in the world.	

Resources for students:
- You and Your Values: http://tiny.cc/G10L1R1
- Choices and Values: http://tiny.cc/G10L1R2

Resources for teachers:
- Values Education Curriculum: http://tiny.cc/G10L2R3
- Activities that Teach Values: http://tiny.cc/G10L2R4
- Lessons and Activities for Teaching Respect: http://tiny.cc/G10L2R5
- Character Education Lesson Plans: http://tiny.cc/G10L2R6
- Advocates for Youth Values Lessons: http://tiny.cc/G10L2R7

> ## Grade 10 Lesson 2
> ## "Community"

Time Frame: 60 minutes | **Subjects**: Social studies |
Designer: Quinn Lockwood
Standards: SDG 1 (End Poverty), 2 (Zero Hunger), 3 (Good Health and Well-Being), 4 (Quality Education), 5 (Gender Equality), 10 (Reduced Inequalities), 16 (Peace, Justice and Strong Institutions), 17 (Partnerships for the Goals)

Summary and Rationale: Students will build on the first lesson in which they thought about their values and identified a problem facing the world that they feel passionate about helping to solve. In this lesson, students will prepare to go out into their local community and conduct interviews with individuals or perhaps several people who are members of an organization that is doing something to fix the problem that the student identified. This can be broadly defined (for example, there might not be someone in the local community doing work that addresses the student's *exact* issue/problem.)

Instructional Goal:

- Teacher will guide students in matching the problem they identified with someone/an organization in their community that is working to address that problem.
- Teacher will help students to develop their own interview protocol and make sure that students are able to practice being an interviewer (using classmates as the interviewees).
- Teacher can discuss issues like recording the interview, making sense of the information they get out of the interview, and how to incorporate interviews into their final paper.

Understanding Goals:

- Students understand the value of talking to people about the work that they do; students understand how to develop questions to ask in the interview.
- Students will also understand how to make connections between the work that people do on a local level and the way this work can impact societal issues.

213

Essential questions:
- What is the purpose of conducting interviews?
- What is the best way to reach out to people and explain what we would like to talk to them about?
- How can we think of questions that answer what we really want to know about the problem we identified?
- How can we make good use of the information that we get from the interviews?
- How can we make sure that we are respectful of others' time?
- What are some challenges that might arise during our interviews?
- What are some strategies we can think of to address those challenges?

Student Learning Objectives (Students Will be Able To):
- Students will develop interview questions
- Students will practice at least one mock interview
- Students will produce a summary of what they found out in the mock interview
- Students will develop a list of questions for their interview with a community member

Assessment: Students will complete mock interviews with classmates, including developing a list of questions and a short write-up of their findings from the interview. Students will submit their interview protocol and questions for the teacher to review before going out into the community to conduct the interview.

Sequence of activities:
- **Teacher preparation:** Before the lesson, teacher should:
  - Identify community partners for students to interview based on the community issues that students identified in the last class. These could include staff at community organizations like homeless shelters or recycling centers, or individuals in the community who are working on various social justice initiatives, like educators, social workers or socially-responsible business people.
  - Students will need to conduct some preliminary research about their topic before they can design effective interview questions. Let students know who their community partner is in advance of this lesson

214

    o   Give students a research assignment to complete before this class that will allow them to have a basic understanding of what their community partner does before attempting to design interview questions.

- **Introduce the topic: (5 mins)** Frame the lesson by letting students know they will be practicing their interviewing skills, as well as getting the chance to put themselves in the shoes of the interviewee. Remind students that in the last class, they explored the idea of values and used their values to identify a problem in their community. Let students know that you (the teacher) have identified some potential partners for students, whether they are organizations or individuals, who are working to address the issues that students raised during the last class. Students will be able to interview these community members and use the information in their final papers. In order to practice for these interviews, let students know they will be able to practice interviewing their classmates.

- **Warm-up activity: (20 minutes)** Start students off with a quick interview practice. Put students into groups of four, and let one pair start while the other pair observes, then swap. Give each pair of students a list of general interview questions and give each pair ten minutes to interview each other (student A for 5 minutes, student B for 5 minutes, then the second pair goes in the same way.) At this point it's not necessary for students to develop their own questions, just to get familiar with asking questions, listening, and taking notes. See the attached resources for the list of sample questions.

- **Reflection/time for feedback: (5 mins)** Give students the opportunity to talk in their group of four about what went well and what could have gone better during the practice interviews. Provide guiding questions for students such as "How did you feel when you were asking the questions? What were some of the challenging things you encountered as the interviewer? How about as the interviewee?"

- **Developing interview questions and protocol: (10 mins)** Pass out the handout with tips and best practices for interviewers. This journalism guide (http://tiny.cc/G10L2R0) from Columbia University, while long, has some pieces that can be taken out and used to create a smaller handout that is appropriate for high school students. Go over the handout with students and let them share ideas about how to use these practices while developing their interview questions.

- **Students frame potential questions for their interviewees and practice: (10 mins)**
  Give each student their assignment/problem and give them the role of the person/organization who is working to address that problem. Give each pair of students a few sample questions and then give them five minutes to develop some sample questions independently. After five minutes of planning, give students five minutes to practice asking and answering the questions.

- **Students share their interview questions with the class and prepare for their next step: (10 minutes)**
  Give students a chance to share their questions and receive feedback from teacher and classmates. As homework, students should expand their list of questions and edit their questions based on feedback they received. Students will be responsible for contacting their community partners to arrange the interview, with support from the teacher as necessary. Let students know that they have the opportunity to arrange phone interviews if in-person interviews are not possible.

Resources for teachers:
- How to Conduct a Journalistic Interview: http://tiny.cc/G10L2R1
- Beyond Questions, Learning the Art of the Interview: http://tiny.cc/G10L2R2

Grade 10 Lesson 3

"Balancing Voices in Global Issues"

Time Frame: 60 minutes | **Subjects:** Social Studies / Geography | **Designer:** Holing Yip

Standards: SDGs 2 (Zero Hunger), 6 (Clean Water and Sanitation), 7 (Affordable and Clean Energy), 8 (Decent Work and Economic Growth), 9 (Industry, Innovation, and Infrastructure), 11 (Sustainable Cities and Communities), 14 (Life Below Water), 15 (Life on Land)

Summary and Rationale: In analysing global events, it is important to recognize that opinions and viewpoints around an issue highly depend on the perspective from which you inspect the issue. In this lesson, using the constructions of large dams around the world as case study, students will be given information from different stakeholder's perspective, and through discuss learn to consider the viewpoints of a wide range of stakeholders.

Instructional Goal:
- Students will practice making evidence-based arguments.
- They will also gain appreciation that differences in opinion often stem from differences in perspectives of different stakeholders.

Understanding Goals:
- Students will understand that different stakeholder perspective breeds different viewpoints and logical conclusions.
- They will also gain the sensitivity to spot and consider the missing voices in a discussion.

Essential questions:
- Who are the stakeholders whose viewpoints are represented in the information packet you read? Who's opinion should bear more weight, and who gets to decide that?
- The arguments from different stakeholders are different, but are they all logical and well-supported?
- Whose voices are not heard?
- How should we consider the interests of non-human creatures?

217

- How should we ensure that more voices are heard?

Student Learning Objectives (Students Will be Able To):
- Students will be able to extrapolate at least two argument are their corresponding supporting evidence from the information packet.
- Students should be able to accurately name the main stakeholders whose opinions are represented in the information packet, and also name at least one stakeholder whose interest is partially represented in the information.
- Students should also be able to name at least one stakeholder whose interest or viewpoint is not present in the information.

Assessment: Teachers will assess:
- the quality of arguments made;
- the evidence used to support the arguments;
- the number and type of stakeholders identified from the information packet;
- the breadth of stakeholders whose voices were not represented that were identified by the students in the last part of the activity.

Sequence of activities:
- Teacher preparation: Before the lesson, the teacher will choose the building of a dam as the discussion topic for the class. The teacher will compile two information packets; information packet A focuses on the government's justification for building the dam and the problems it seeks to solve; information packet B focuses on the perspective of inhabitants who will be affected and displaced by the dams.
- (5 min) In the beginning of the lesson, the teacher will ask the students to be divided into small groups of 3-4. The teacher will explain that the lesson is to build student's ability to back up their arguments with evidence, and that a country previously had plans to build a dam but a new government leader is assuming office and wants to reevaluate the dam project. The student groups' task is to advise the new government leader what his next step should be.
- (2 min) Students are divided small groups of 3-4 students. Half of the groups will receive information packet A, while the other half will receive information packet B. The students are not informed that there are two sets of information packets.

- (13 min) Students, in small groups, come up with three arguments for their advice to the new government leader, and backed the argument up by evidence or viewpoints found in the information packet.
- (15 min) Student groups then present their argument and evidence to the whole class.
- (5 min) Teacher discuss with the class the major difference in the advice given by different student groups The teacher reveals to the students that different groups have been given information packets that are from the perspectives of different stakeholders.
- (10 min) Student groups merge to form larger groups so each new, large group has both students who read information packet A and students who read information packet B. The students discuss to identify the stakeholders whose perspectives and interests are represented in each information packet, and share this with the whole class.
- (10 min) Students then brainstorm in small groups or as a whole class the stakeholders whose full perspectives may not have been represented in either information packet. They also discuss whose perspective they most personally identify with, and why.

Resources for students:
- Google map and Google Earth to inspect the dams

Resources for teachers:
- China's Three Gorges Dam: http://tiny.cc/G10L3R1
  The River Educator's Toolkit: http://tiny.cc/G10L3R2
  Modern China, the Dam Debate: http://tiny.cc/G10L3R3
- Cost-Benefit Analysis - China Dam: http://tiny.cc/G10L3R4
  Three Gorges Dam, A Catastrophe?: http://tiny.cc/G10L3R5
- Ethiopia's Gibe III Dam: http://tiny.cc/G10L3R6
  International Rivers, Gibe III: http://tiny.cc/G10L3R7
  Uneasy Choice: Where do We Stand on Gibe III: http://tiny.cc/G10L3R8
  Brazil's Belo Monte Dam: http://tiny.cc/G10L3R9
  Massive Dam Project Strikes Heart of Amazon: http://tiny.cc/G10L3R10

Fernando M. Reimers et al.

Grade 10 Lesson 4

"World"

Time Frame: 60 minutes | **Subjects:** Social Studies |
Designer: Eva Flavia Martinez Orbegozo
Standards: All 17

Summary and Rationale: In this lesson, students will connect the local problems they have identified and with which they have worked in the previous lessons to the SDGs.

Instructional Goal: Students will gain understanding of how global issues are connected to local problems and reflect on how their interest and knowledge about them can inform solutions.

Understanding Goals:
- Local issues can be a manifestation of global problems.
- Local solutions may have a larger impact.
- Individuals can play a role in improving the world by being aware of global problems, knowing how they are reflected in their local context and by being involved in finding solutions.

Essential questions:
- How are the problems on which students have been working related to the different SDGs?
- Which of the solutions explored through community interviews and research could potentially be adapted to other contexts? Which one could be seen as global solutions? What are the reasons why they could work? What would be possible problems in other contexts?
- How does the understanding of the problem in which students have worked change when learning about SDGs?

Student Learning Objectives (Students Will be Able To):
- Students will be able to connect local problems to the SDGs by linking each of their problems to the SDGs to which they relate. They will need to justify these connections.

221

- Students will be able to navigate between the local and global contexts by assessing the potential validity of the solutions they have encountered in previous sessions in other contexts in the world.
- Students will be able to communicate the connection between local and global and the possible difficulties when translating solutions in between contexts.

Assessment: News broadcast written and enacted in groups (and if possible, recorded).

Sequence of activities:
- **Introduction (Feel):**
  - **Example of a successful local solution:**
  - Students are shown a video about using plastic bottles filled with water and bleach to light up houses with no natural light or electricity. Link to video: https://www.youtube.com/watch?v=cQCHvO2H0_0 *(If there is no possibility to show the video, the story can be narrated and a few pictures can be shown)*

  - **Discussion and reflection:** The teacher ask students to consider the following questions (first in pairs and then in a whole group discussion):

    - What are the different problems this solution is trying to address? (Examples: lack of electricity)
    - What are the big causes for those problems? (Example: poverty)
    - The teacher can write down problems and causes that have to do with the SDGs (i.e. poverty, affordable and clean energy, sustainable cities…)

- **THINK:**
  - **Introduction to the SDGs**: The teacher should introduce the SDGs paying attention to context.
  - **Connection between local problems and SDGs**: Students are asked to think about the problems they have heard about and students identify problems which related to their community and the previous session. Students answer the question:

- 'How is your problem connected to the SDGs? Identify all the different
      SDGs to which your problem is connected.
  - The teacher will post headings with the name of each SDG on the walls around the classroom. Students will have small cards or post-its with the name of their problem and they need to decide under which SDGs they can place their problem. Students go around the classroom and post their problem under as many SDGs as they consider possible. The last two minutes of this activity will be used for the teacher to ask a few students to justify and explain how their problem relates to the SDGs they have chosen.
    - *Teacher can ask students to discuss the following questions in pairs:* What problem did you pick? Can you describe the problem? Who is affected by this problem? How do we know? Which SDGs strive to address this problem? How do they address it?

- **ACT:**
  - **News broadcast on SDGs and local problem:**
  - Preparation: Students will be asked to script a news broadcast which includes the following:
    - What problem did you pick?
    - Can you describe the problem?
    - Who is affected by this problem? How do we know?
    - Which SDGs strive to address this problem? How do they address it?
    - What can we do in our community to help address this problem?

    * Students need to write the script as if they were reporting to their community news station - students need to cover the news of this problem and the call to action to solve the problem.

    Recording of broadcast (if possible) and playing them for the classroom. Alternatively they can just enact them in front of the classroom.

Resources for students:
- Teacher guidance,
- SDGs website (or printouts with the goals),

223

- Class notes and
- Deliverables from previous session.

Resources for teachers:
- SDGs website

Grade 10 Lesson 5

"Capstone"

Time Frame: 60 minutes (multiple lessons) | **Subjects:** Language writing, Social Studies
Designer: Madhuri Dhariwal

Standards: All 17 are relevant to this lesson

Summary and Rationale:
The students will put together the research they have conducted in the first 4 lessons, to produce one paper, with the aim of publishing it.

Instructional Goal:
- Students will be able to collate their writing into one cohesive piece.
- Students will be able to edit their own work.
- Students will be able to build a connection between themselves, their immediate surroundings, the world at large, and their role in solving world problems.

Understanding Goals:
- The world is interconnected.
- Little actions can have big impacts.
- Conducting research is essential and involves a process.

Essential questions:
- How do we tie together different pieces of research?
- What is 'my' role in solving problems in the world?

Student Learning Objectives (Students Will be Able To):
- Understand the connection between the values they hold and the problems they identify in their surroundings.
- Check whether the problems they think exist, actually exist in their community.
- Write papers of varying lengths for each lesson.
- Work collaboratively

Assessment: Students will present a well-researched, well articulated final project which demonstrates their understanding of various global challenges and potential solutions.

Sequence of activities:

- **Opening and setting up: (5 minutes)**
  Explain that the students have to create one paper, building on the work they have done in the past 4 lessons.

- **Discussion about the paper framework: (10 minutes)**
  Provide an outline of the framework for the paper:
  - Introduction and statement of problem (what is the problem)
  - Methods Section (talking about the different methods - interviews, secondary sources, main concepts discussed)
  - How do you know it's a problem? Why is it a problem?
  - Main ideas drawn from the interviews
  - Research on the positive deviant
  - Relation to a world problem.
  - Proposed solution/s.
  - References
  - Appendices
  Alternative:
  The research can be presented as in any creative writing format - a story, picture boards, poetry etc.
- **Starting to collate: (30 minutes)**
  Within their respective groups, the students will start to put together the work they have done. They will then break up the work among themselves and have a rough draft by the end of class.

- **Presenting to the class (10 minutes)**
  Each group will present to the entire class: their problem statement, the proposed solution, in 1-2 minutes.

- **Next Steps (5 minutes):**
  The students will be asked to refine their work at home and submit the draft within the next week.

The teacher will review the drafts, hand them back with feedback and the students will revise and submit. The teacher can then talk to the Principal or by try her/himself to get the papers published as a combined book. The students can also be involved in the process.

Grade 11

Lesson Overview	
Learning Goal	
In Grade 11, students will focus different aspects of gender: stereotypes, the role gender plays in everyday life, and it's impact on larger global dynamics. Then, students will learn about the concept of positive deviance, and learn how they can promote change by identifying and supporting positive deviance in their own lives.	
Lesson Scaffold	
Lesson 1	**Gender and Stereotypes**
Lesson 2	**Gender in Everyday Life**
Lesson 3	**Global Conversations About Gender**
Lesson 4	**Identifying Positive Deviance**
Lesson 5	**Project Presentation and Reflection**
Learning Objectives	

- Students will learn about stereotypes and explore how they can be harmful to people.
- Students will engage with conversations about gender on a global scale.
- Students learn about positive deviance and how to identify it in their own lives.

Grade 11 Lesson 1

"Introduction to gender and sex; identity; gender roles; stereotypes attached to gender, and LGBTQ (if context appropriate)"

Time Frame for each Lesson: 60 minutes | **Subjects**:: Civics, History, Social Studies |
Designers: Isabelle Byusa, Arianna Pattek, Emily Pope, Sam (Shiv) Sharma, Tisha Verma and Devon Wilson

Standards: SDG 5: Gender Equality

Summary and Rationale: This lesson is designed to understand the difference between gender and sex, identity, and the stereotypes attached to gender. Students will examine UNESCO's gender glossary and will examine how they have encountered or observed gendered roles in their own experiences. They will then go on to imagine what gender equality might look like in their context.

Instructional Goal: Promote higher level thinking skills in a scaffolded manner. Students will examine how these concepts are seen in daily life and will add to these definitions in order to enrich them or contextualize them.

Understanding:
Through the lense of their lived experience, students will understand the difference and draw connections between: Gender and Sex | Gender Equality and Gender Equity

Essential questions:
- What is the difference between gender and sex?
- How would you define masculinity and femininity?
- What confines do these definitions entail?
- What is the difference between equity and equality?
- What is the pathway forward?

231

Student Learning Objectives (Students Will be Able To):

- Students will understand the difference between and gain the vocabulary to discuss gender and sex, Gender Equality and Gender Equity.
- Students will draw connections between these concepts and their lived experience.

Assessment: Students will be able to participate in class and small group discussion based upon the the topics covered above in the Student Learning Objectives.

Sequence of Activities:
- Students read relevant definitions from UNESCO's Gender Mainstreaming Implementation Framework as homework before class.
- Class begins with the TED Talk "We should all be feminists" by Chimamanda Ngozi Adichie
- Discuss the video and integrate the UNESCO definitions into the discussion
- Next, have students write and reflect about how they see gender or gendered roles in their daily lives, and what gender equality might look like in their context
- Students will discuss their thoughts in small groups - painting a picture of gendered roles and proposing a path towards gender equality
- The teacher will facilitate a broad discussion with the whole class on these topics.

Resources for teachers:
- UNESCO's Gender Mainstreaming Implementation Framework: http://tiny.cc/G11L1R1
- (Video) "We should all be feminists" TED Talk by Chimamanda Ngozi Adichie: http://tiny.cc/G11L1R2
- From where I Stand - A Gender Equality Project: http://tiny.cc/G11L1R3
- UNESCO Gender Equality Tools: http://tiny.cc/G11L1R4

Grade 11 Lesson 2

"Community Based Research - Gender Dynamics in My Community"

Time Frame for each Lesson: 60 minutes | **Subjects::** Civics, History, Social Studies |
Designers: Isabelle Byusa, Arianna Pattek, Emily Pope, Sam (Shiv) Sharma, Tisha Verma and Devon Wilson

Standards: SDG 5: Gender Equality

Summary and Rationale: Encourage students to understand their personal relationship to gender dynamics and how gender dynamics play out in their own community

Instructional Goals: Provide students with tools to conduct community-based research around gender dynamics and gender roles

Understanding Goals: How issues of gender manifest in different aspects of everyday life

Essential questions:
- Are jobs in your community divided by gender?
- Can women participate in the same activities as men?
- Are there distinct roles in your family divided by gender?

Student Learning Objectives (Students Will be Able To):
- Conduct research in order to understand the gender makeup of their community

Assessment: Turn in a Community Gender Profile - listing jobs in their community and the number of women and men who work in each job

Sequence of Activities:

- **Pre-Class (15min):** Emma Watson at HeForShe Campaign (Video)
  http://tiny.cc/G11L2R1

Fernando M. Reimers et al.

- o Watch the He For She campaign speech by Emma Watson (depending on your lesson time- can watch whole speech or chosen clips)
- o In pairs students discuss what they think the call to action in the video is and why it is important (2 mins)
- o Teacher leads class discussion on students' reflections on the video and introduces the importance of individual responsibility and community engagement. (5 mins)

- **Prep for research activity (20min):**
  Whole class discussion about conducting community based research. Develop a list of questions to explore in their community. Examples: are there more women or men who own business? Is there anyone in your community who defies gender stereotypes? If so, how? Talk to them about this experience. Additionally, ask men and women in their professions about how they got that job (Did they choose? Did they do it because their mother/father did it? etc) (Within their family, what do they want to explore? Talk to your parents about their roles in the family.)

- **Small group work (15min):**
  Develop their community gender profiles in small groups. Develop a list of questions in small groups and a research plan (where will we go first? Who will we talk to?)

- **Conclusion/wrap up (10min):**
  Students share what they developed in their small groups

Resources for students:
- Emma Watson at HeForShe Campaign (Video) http://tiny.cc/G11L2R1
- International Labor Organization Framework for Gender Analysis and Planning: http://tiny.cc/G11L2R2

Grade 11 Lesson 3

"Tying it All Together - The Final Product"

Time Frame for each Lesson: 60 minutes | **Subjects:**: Civics, History, Social Studies |
Designers: Isabelle Byusa, Arianna Pattek, Emily Pope, Sam (Shiv) Sharma, Tisha Verma and Devon Wilson

Standards: SDG 5: Gender Equality

Summary and Rationale: Engage students in a conversation about gender status around the world and open their eyes beyond their community

Instructional Goal: To give students the opportunity to further develop their vocabulary and thinking around gender issues in a global context

Understanding Goals: Status of women and gender minorities around the world

Essential questions:
- What is the situation of women across the globe?

Student Learning Objectives (Students Will be Able To):
- To familiarize themselves with the situation of women across the globe.
- To analyze gender inequity across contexts.

Assessment: Participation in the class and small group discussions

Sequence of Activities:
- Students are assigned a region around the world: Scandinavia, Europe, North America, Latin America, North Africa and the Middle East, South Asia, Southeast Asia, East Asia, Sub-saharan Africa, etc. and are assigned an identity: Women, Men, Lesbian/Gay, Transgender, etc. Students will conduct research on the educational, career, and social freedoms their group has in 3 regions.
- Students will compile a report and present to the class

- Students debrief on their reflections. What did they find that was surprising? How did this change their view of gender inequity?

Resources for students:
- Students conduct their own independent research

Resources for teachers:
- Guide students to various resources in order to enhance the quality of the presentation
- Workshop Activity for Gender Equity Simulation: http://tiny.cc/G11L3R1
- Book Review: Worlds Apart: http://tiny.cc/G11L3R2

Grade 11 Lesson 4

"Positive Deviants on Gender Equity, Stereotypes or LGBTQ Rights"

Time Frame for each Lesson: 60 minutes | **Subjects::** Civics, History, Social Studies |
Designers: Isabelle Byusa, Arianna Pattek, Emily Pope, Sam (Shiv) Sharma, Tisha Verma and Devon Wilson

Standards: SDG 5: Gender Equality

Summary and Rationale: Students will be asked to explore a topic of gender roles, gender stereotypes, or LGBTQ rights in greater depth. Through this process, students will be challenged to develop their research, writing and editing skills.

Instructional Goal: provide students with tools to conduct community-based research around gender dynamics and gender roles

Understanding Goals: How people are working to develop gender equity in various contexts around the world.

Essential Questions:
- How do gender roles and gender stereotypes manifest themselves in our day to day lives?
- What is gender equality and equity?
- How can individuals address these issues?

Student Learning Objectives (Students Will be Able To):
Research and write on a topic of gender equity.

Assessment: Students final piece of written work - assessment can be completed outside of class.

Sequence of Activities:

- Students will be asked to reflect on the gender equity issues that surprised them the most during the first three lessons. (5 minutes)
- From here, students will be challenged to a.) Conduct greater research on the problem and it's sources, and b.) Research people or projects that may already be in play to counteract that problem (locally and/or internationally). (remaining class time)
- After conducting initial research, students may either start work on writing a piece on one of the people or projects they discovered and post their final work to blog (this opportunity could be used to create a class blog, or a specific blog on the topic of gender equity), alternatively, if students are unable to find very much on the issue, they can create a proposal on a project to counter the issue. (outside of class time)
- At the end of the project, students will be challenged to think about their research on their topic and complete a "I used to think _____, I now think _____" reflection activity. More information on these resources are included in the resources for teachers section below. (outside of class time)

Resources for teachers:
- Visible Thinking Framework – Project Zero: http://tiny.cc/G11L4R1

Grade 11 Lesson 5

" Capstone Action Project - Contributing to a Gender Blind Community"

Time Frame for each Lesson: 60 minutes | **Subjects:**: Civics, History, Social Studies |

Designers: Isabelle Byusa, Arianna Pattek, Emily Pope, Sam (Shiv) Sharma, Tisha Verma and Devon Wilson

Standards: SDG 5: Gender Equality

Summary and Rationale: Engage students to boldly envision a gender blind world, a world in which your gender does not decide what you can do and achieve in life

Instructional Goal: Provide students with tools to independently explore and act on issues of gender equity.

Understanding Goals: We all should strive towards building a gender blind world

Essential questions:
- Why can we not boldly dream of a gender blind society?
- Why are we letting our gender determine what we can and cannot achieve in life?

Student Learning Objectives (Students Will be Able To):
To conduct research in order to understand the gender makeup of their community - and develop competencies related to "taking action" based upon their research.

Assessment: Submitted research project

Sequence of Activities:
- Continue discussion of students findings from lesson 4 and the topic of a "gender blind society". (5-10 minutes)

239

- Based upon research conducted and shared in lesson 4, students will be challenged to make an action plan that would allow for a more equitable society. (remaining classtime)
- Students may conduct personal interviews in order to learn different points of view on gender equity and proposed action plans. (optional: outside of class)
- Students envision the short term and long term impact of their programs and how a world might look when there is gender equality and a world which is gender blind (10 minutes after completion of project)

Resources for students:
- Students conduct their own independent research

Resources for teachers:
- Guide students to various resources in order to enhance the quality of their research paper

Grade 12

Lesson Overview	
Learning Goal	
In Grade 12, students will focus on how they can apply all the knowledge they have gained over the past twelve years when they are no longer students. They will explore opportunities for affecting positive change in their careers, service, and everyday lives, and will leave inspired to continue working to better the world.	
Lesson Scaffold	
Lesson 1	The Role of Service
Lesson 2	Careers: What is my place in the world?
Lesson 3	The Role of Institutions in Modern Society
Lesson 4	Take, Make, Waste: A Sustainable Economic Paradigm
Lesson 5	Doing Good : Catalyzing local impact to make the world a better place
Learning Objectives	

- Students will formulate plans for after they finish high schools.
- Students will think critically about how they can apply all the lessons they have learned once they have left school.
- Students will be inspired to continue creating positive change as adults.

Grade 12 Lesson 1

"The Role of Service"

Time Frame: 60 Minutes | **Subjects:** Social Studies, English Language Arts
Designer: Somoh Supharukchinda, with Alexandra Ball, Deaweh Benson, Heer Shaikh, and Nicolás Riveros
Standards: No Poverty; Reduced inequalities; Partnerships for the Goals

Summary and Rationale:

- In this lesson, students will consider the role that service plays in improving people's lives and the planet. They will be introduced to selected examples of service and explore tools used in conducting a needs assessment and developing a response to the need.
- Students will make a case for a recipient to receive an "Exemplary Service" award and present their recommendations. Examples in this lesson are selected nominees from *CNN Heroes*, but teachers may use a different source that reflects individuals from their own contexts.

Instructional Goal:

- Introduce students to tools for conducting a needs assessment and developing a program or project to respond to these needs
- Encourage/inspire their advocacy and agency in serving their communities
- Provide an opportunity to practice presentation and persuasion skills

Standards:

- ***Ethical and Intercultural Orientation (Feeling)***
  - ○ Learn how to be a good person
- ***Knowledge and Skills (Thinking)***
  - ○ Apply knowledge across subjects demonstrating a deeper understanding of Content.
  - ○ Acquire skills in economics and financial relations, science, technology, data analysis, and health that will allow students to address real world issues
  - ○ Analyze and researching solutions to problems (water, energy, and food) from the perspectives of different roles, such as consumers, businesses, scientists, policy makers,

243

researchers, retailers, media, and development cooperation agencies, among others.

- ***Agency and Empowerment (Acting)***
  - o Students will acquire a pragmatic set of skills that instills them with a sense of agency.
  - o Students should orient their future career goals toward placing value on the ethical foundations they have learned
  - o Self-Efficacy: balance skills of independence/autonomy and ability to work in teams
  - o Ability to communicate ideas
- ***Agency and Empowerment (Acting)***
  - o Create empowered students to create change (social change makers/ entrepreneurial leaders)

Understanding:
Individuals have personal agency in improving their communities and world through service activities/projects. Effective service addresses a community need, using strategic tools to develop an appropriate response and measure impact.

Essential questions:
- What are examples of ways in which an individual can serve their community?
- What tools are useful in developing a service activity or project? How will I know if my service activity or project is improving lives?
- How can I strengthen my community and world through service?

Student Learning Objectives (Students Will be Able To):
Students will be able to
- Identify examples of service activities and projects
- Use strategic tools to understand a community's needs and develop a service activity or project
- Make a persuasive case for why a service activity or project improves his/her community or world
- Articulate their personal commitment to improving their communities through service

Assessment: (Optional) Assign students to write a persuasive essay as homework. The essay should argue in favor of one of the nominees, using the tools of the class to explain why they selected the individual they did for the

"Exemplary Service" Award. The teacher can share the top 3 nominees and an accompanying synopsis of arguments in a subsequent class.

Sequence of Activities:

- **(5 mins) Introduce the lesson and identify community problems**
  - Explain to class that this lesson will focus on identifying problems, potential solutions, and tools to identify both of these components.
  - Share an example problem (e.g., the local playground is littered). Ask students for examples of other issues/problems that they've observed in their communities.
  - Share an example solution (e.g., a local volunteer clean-up program). Ask students for some ideas of how they might address the problems they identified.

- **(10 mins) Overview needs assessment tools**
  - Give brief lecture on examples of tools that social scientists use to understand community needs and develop solutions. Provide examples such as a needs assessment, logic model, or theory of change (see student and teacher resources).
  - Walk students through the application of one of these tools to one of the examples that you or students identified as a problem.

- **(5 mins) Introduce main activity**
  - Share with students that many others have dedicated a portion of their lives to addressing these types of community problems through service activities and projects. Today they will learn about some of these individuals through the stories told on "CNN Heroes," which recognizes selected individuals through an annual awards ceremony.
  - Break students into small groups (4-5 students) and assign them to a "CNN Heroes" nominee.
  - Instruct students to:
    - View a video clip and any accompanying information on their assigned "CNN Hero." This may include additional online research.
    - Using the tools from class:
      - Identify the problem that the individual was seeking to address

- Identify the solution that the individual pursued
- Identify the results of the service initiative/project
- Prepare a 3-minute presentation on why their nominee deserves the CNN Heroes Award
- Optional: Preview the homework assignment (see Assessment) to encourage students to take notes during the presentation

- **(25 mins)** Groups view videos of their nominee, conduct research, and prepare for their presentations
- **(15 mins)** Groups present their nominees to the class

Resources for students
- CNN Heroes: http://tiny.cc/G12L1R1

Resources for teachers
- Planning a Needs Assessment (p. 5 onward): http://tiny.cc/G12L1R2
- (Chapter 1)
- Kellogg Foundation Logic Model Guide: http://tiny.cc/G12L1R3
- Center for Theory of Change: http://tiny.cc/G12L1R4
- A Practical Tool for Action, Theory of Change: http://tiny.cc/G12L1R5

Grade 12 Lesson 2

"Careers: What is my place in the world?"

Time Frame: 60 Minutes | **Subjects:** Social Studies, Communications, Writing |
Designer: Abimbola Adetunji

Standards: Decent work and economic growth; industry, innovation, and infrastructure.

Summary and Rationale:
- Students often times either self-censor their future possibilities or are not actively involved in deciding their career paths. This lesson seeks to help graduating students consider possible future careers and how these careers might impact their immediate and global environment.
- In this lesson, students will consider their likes, dislikes, interests and passions and how these might be infused into different occupations. The aim is that this lesson will help students explore careers and the agency they possess to change the world.
- Students will present career options explaining why they have chosen this career, its impact on their lives, on the world around them, and in the global context, as well as what additional skills they will require to be effective in this chosen career path.

Instructional Goal:
- To facilitate self-reflection among students and create a foundation to help students define their life purpose
- To encourage their agency to shape the world
- To provide an opportunity to practice research, and writing skills

Standards:

- ***Ethical and Intercultural Orientation (Feeling)***
  - Recognize and appreciate the interdependence of all people, living things, and the planet
  - Understand the rights of all humans to lead happy, healthy, and productive lives regardless of gender, age, disability, etc. (no poverty, no hunger, etc)

247

- o Express self through arts (including philosophical expression)

- **Knowledge and Skills (Thinking)**
  - o Question the existing power structures and be aware of their place within a specific world context
  - o Understand one's own identity and roots, others' identities and roots, how cultures shape identities, and where one is situated in space and time (Self-Awareness)
  - o Demonstrate awareness of actions and responsibilities in an interconnected context (Global Citizenship); Project Zero resource: investigate the world, recognise perspectives
  - o Apply knowledge across subjects demonstrating a deeper understanding of content.
  - o Understand the elements of trust and collaboration, decent and gainful employment, and why it is important to making and sustaining relationships both locally and globally.
  - o Be aware of the well-being of the self and society (physical, mental, spiritual, etc.)
  - o Acquire skills in economics and financial relations, science, technology, data analysis, and health that will allow students to address real world issues
  - o Analyze and researching solutions to problems (water, energy, and food) from the perspectives of different roles, such as consumers, businesses, scientists, policy makers, researchers, retailers, media, and development cooperation agencies, among others.

- **Agency and Empowerment (Acting)**
  - o Students should orient their future career goals toward placing value on the ethical foundations they have learned
  - o Have the agency to act with resilience and a sense of possibility, recognize and challenge injustice, commit to overcoming adversity, plan/carry out an activism project of choice
  - o Ability to be innovative
  - o Ability to communicate ideas
  - o Ability to be engaged and proactive
  - o Belief that improvements can be made through growth mindset

    ○   Create empowered students to create change (social change makers/ entrepreneurial leaders)

Understanding:

There are multiple careers in the world that require different skills and there is a career for me. It is my duty to shape the world positively and I can define how I want to do this. I don't have to choose between a great career and my passion/interests; I can have both and be happy. These are the next steps I need to make to succeed in my chosen career and these are the skills I will require. This is how I can impact the world.

Essential questions:

- What do I like/dislike?
- What annoys me the most about my world? Why?
- What would my ideal world look like?
- Which of the SDGs play a role in this ideal world? How?
- What role would I play in this ideal world?
- What are my favorite school subjects? Why?
- What are my hobbies? Why?
- What careers incorporate my favorite subjects and the things i like?
- If I want to be _____ these are the skills i need
- How can I achieve this goal?
- How will it change my life, my immediate environment, and the world?
- What can I start to do now?

Student Learning Objectives (Students Will be Able To):

- The different career options available on a global scale
- Their own underlying interests and where these intersect with obtainable careers
- That they possess the agency to impact the world
- That a future career can be joyful even with the responsibilities.
- Creating an action plan

Assessment: Students will write a 1,500 word "statement of purpose" that answers all the essential questions and explains the resources they will require. Essay should be graded on a 5 point scale for specificity (1), clearness of argument and thoughtfulness (1), innovation in proposed impact (1), Use of examples and analogies to support argument (1), and action plan (1).

Sequence of Activities:
(NOTE - this activity can also be facilitated by any professional in academic and non-academic settings)

- **(5 minutes) Introduction**
    - Teacher asks 3 students for own definition of a career.
    - Following this, teacher defines career and explains difference between a career and a job
        - *Career: an occupation undertaken for a significant period of a person's life and with opportunities for progress*
        - *Difference between a career and a job:* *A* **career** *is the pursuit of a lifelong ambition or the general course of progression towards lifelong goals.* **Job** *is an activity through which an individual can earn money. It is a regular activity in exchange of payment*

- **Class discussion (5 minutes)**
    - Teacher asks students to discuss work activities they know and classify these into jobs and careers - within small groups for 2 minutes and as a class for 3 minutes.

- **Teacher shares (10 minutes)**
    - Teacher explains own career journey to becoming a teacher, highlighting the interests, vision, and steps taken to achieve this goal. Explains challenges and highlights agency to overcome challenges. Defines how this career has impacted their life, immediate community and global community, tying these back to any applicable SDGs.

- **Self reflection (10 minutes)**
    - Teacher writes the essential questions on the board and asks students to self-reflect and answer these question.
    - Teacher collects notes.

- **Teacher leads discussion on students notes (10 minutes)**
    - Facilitate conversation on what questions were easy to answer and why? What questions were difficult to answer and why?

- o Ask students to think of a difficult situation or problem they have experienced and what knowledge or skills helped to solve this?
- o Invite a willing student to share.

- **Teacher leads discussion on "My ideal world" (10 minutes)**
  - o Facilitate conversation on characteristics of an ideal world juxtaposing these ideals against the challenges in the real world.
  - o How do the SDGs play a role in shaping this ideal world?
  - o Invite a willing student to share their vision for an ideal world and their role in creating or shaping it.

- **Conclusion and assignment (5 minutes)**
  - o Teacher recaps, discussing examples that have been discussed that highlight agency to overcome difficult situations.
  - o Teacher explains "Statement of Purpose" assignment, explaining grading rubric and expectations.

Resources for students:
- Conduct informational interviews of 5 diverse members of your community and seek to understand their career choices.
- If available, visit your school career and guidance counsellor.
- Career Test: http://tiny.cc/G12L2R1
- Career Outlook: http://tiny.cc/G12L2R2
- My Future: http://tiny.cc/G12L2R3

Resources for teachers:
- Career and College Readiness: http://tiny.cc/G12L2R4
- Career Exploration: http://tiny.cc/G12L2R5
- Grade 12 Career Guidance Lesson PLans: http://tiny.cc/G12L2R6
- 4 Fun Career Planning Activities for Secondary Students: http://tiny.cc/G12L2R7
- Career and Academic Connections: http://tiny.cc/G12L2R8

Fernando M. Reimers et al.

Grade 12 Lesson 3

"The Role of Institutions in Modern Society"

Time Frame: 45 Minutes | **Subjects:** History, Government & Politics
Designer: Deaweh Benson, Alexandra Ball, with Somoh Supharukchinda, Heer Shaikh, and Nicolás Riveros

Standards: Peace, Justice, and Strong Institutions; Reduced Inequalities

Summary and Rationale: In this lesson, students will consider the role that institutions play in effecting societal change and individual lives. In this sample, the institution the students will learn about is the national government; however, this lesson can be adjusted to address any other institution (financial institutions, universities, local or state governments, private enterprises, etc.)

Instructional Goal: To use examples from history to facilitate discussions of how individual relate to institutions, and how institutions shape societies.

Standards:

- *Ethical and Intercultural Orientation (Feeling)*
  - Cultivate an appreciation, curiosity, and respect for cultural diversity and world culture as the foundation for self-reflection, identity formation, and empathetically approaching human interaction.

- *Knowledge and Skills (Thinking)*
  - Question the existing power structures and be aware of their place within a specific world context
  - Recognize cultural prejudice and the ability to minimize its effect
  - Analyze and researching solutions to problems (water, energy, and food) from the perspectives of different roles, such as consumers, businesses, scientists, policy makers, researchers, retailers, media, and development cooperation agencies, among others.

- *Agency and Empowerment (Acting)*
  - Create empowered students to create change (social change makers/ entrepreneurial leaders)

Understanding:
Institutions operate with autonomy, with their own values and interest, and have a real impact on the lives of individuals; as a citizen, it is my duty to be aware of the factors that might influence institutional responses to changing social circumstances, and to understand my personal capacity to affect change.

Essential questions:
- How do institutions respond to changing societal circumstances and affect the lives of individuals?

Student Learning Objectives (Students Will be Able To):
- Institutions operate with autonomy, with their own values and interest, and have a real impact the lives of individuals
- These institutional responses may or may not align with the needs and wishes of the public, and it is up to individuals to be aware/skeptical of all institutional actions.

Assessment: While there is no formal assessment for this lesson, teachers should make sure that all individuals are participating in group discussion and help to produce a final response on how they would have responded differently.

Sequence of Activities:

- **Introduction (5 minutes)**
  Teacher writes the definition of an institution on the board, and students each write down as many examples of institutions as they can think of.

  Institution: A society or organization founded for a political, religious, educational, social, or similar purpose; an established organization having an important role in the life of a country.

- **Teacher collects responses** and writes all relevant answers on the board **(5 minutes)**

254

- **Teacher gives a brief lecture** on governmental response to a challenging moment in history. **(10 minutes)**
  This can be any historical moment relevant to the schools' given cultural context; for this example, we have included resources related to the US Government's response to the civil rights movement.

- **Teacher leads discussion** on what went well with the governmental response or what could have been better. **(5 minutes)**

- **Teacher facilitates small group sessions** of students 'rewriting history.' Students work together to decide how they would approach the challenge differently. **(15 minutes)**

- **Each group shares what they decided. (5 minutes)**

Resources for teachers:
- Lesson Plans for Civil Rights, White House: http://tiny.cc/G12L3R1
- Civil Rights - Ferguson: http://tiny.cc/G12L3R2
- Global Nonviolent Action Database: http://tiny.cc/G12L3R3

Grade 12 Lesson 4

"Take, Make, Waste: A Sustainable Economic Paradigm"

Time Frame: 1-2 Class Periods | **Subjects:** Economics, Social Studies & Entrepreneurship
Designer: Nicolás Riveros with Alexandra Ball, Deaweh Benson, Heer Shaikh, Somoh Supharukchinda.

Standards: SDG 12 - Responsible Consumption and Production

Summary and Rationale: Students graduating from school will have to (continue to) make decisions as consumers and producers in an increasingly interconnected global economy throughout their lives. When thinking about a sustainable world for future generations and ourselves, considering the impact of the mainstream economic model of production and progress in the world is worthwhile. Currently, a considerable number of goods are disposed as waste after consumption. With continuously reduced product life cycles, the rate at which waste is being generated is increasing. This situation not only generates an efficiency problem (resources are being depleted faster and disposed without using them completely), but poses a major challenge for sustainability of life in the planet as a whole.

Teachers are encouraged to redesign the lesson in whatever way better serves the context and particular characteristics of the students in their classes.

Instructional Goal: Forge an ethical orientation towards the use of resources in the world and understand our responsibility to preserve/conserve our planet for sustainability.

Understanding:
- Students will be invited to challenge some of the ideas that underlie the mainstream economic model of production/progress in the world.
- The key concept to learn from this lesson is the idea of a *circular economy*.

257

- The model of a circular economy is a proposal to help reshape production and consumption patterns in the world, aiming to reduce the amount of waste and trash that is generated globally.

Essential questions:
- How do our patterns of consumption impact the world?
- What alternatives can we think of, design, and implement to change the current trends of amount of waste generated in the world?

Student Learning Objectives (Students Will Understand that):
- Current patterns of production and consumption pose a threat to the sustainability of life in the world.
- There are alternatives to reshape the economic model of production/progress (and we will explore just one of them).
- In their personal, professional, and civic lives, they will have the opportunity to bring about change to the economic model of production/progress, helping develop a more sustainable approach towards the use of resources in the world.

Assessment: The activity does not require a formal assessment, but teachers can provide feedback and formative evaluation to students considering: their engagement during the group activities, their participation in group discussions, and the relevance of the ideas shared. The final product of the lesson (mosaic) can a be assessed in terms of quality, breadth, and creativity.

Sequence of Activities:
* For this activity students will work in small groups (4 to 6 students preferably).

- **Our own experience and previous knowledge: time for group reflection (20 mins)**
  - Prior to the session, students should complete or build a chart with information related to some goods they or their families might have owned/acquired in the past years (ideally including those bought before high school). The minimum information required is the number of items bought or acquired by the student or his/her family. Additional useful information includes year of purchase or acquisition of the good. No information about prices or brands is needed. The types of goods to be included in the chart are: i) mobile phones; ii) televisions; iii) radios (or music player devices).

In class, each student will share with their group the information gathered previous to the session. Together the group has to calculate the total and average number of goods, for each type of device, they or their families have used in the agreed-upon time frame.

Considering the individual and final report numbers, students will engage in discussing the following questions:
- What are the similarities or differences in the patterns of use/consumption of the reported goods? (e.g., which goods have been bought more, which goods are more common amongst us, etc.).
- Are any of these goods being bought more frequently by us, our families, or the people we know?
- Are all these goods still under use by us or our families?
- What happens to the goods we no longer use? Where are they now? Do we keep them, sell them, dispose them?
- What happens to the disposed goods? Do we know if they are used again or if they are just regarded as waste?

- **Exploring new ideas: time to take part in a current debate (15 mins)**
  - Watch together as whole group one of the following videos:
    - (Video) Can a Circular Economy Make Trash Obsolete?: http://tiny.cc/G12L4R1
    - (Video) The Circular Economy: http://tiny.cc/g12L4R2
    - (Video) Sustainability through a circular economy: http://tiny.cc/G12L4R3
    - (Video) Re-thinking Progress: The Circular Economy: http://tiny.cc/G12L4R4
  - Share reactions and comments on the video. Questions that might be asked in order to engage students in this section include:

- What are the main characteristics of a linear/circular economy?
- How can the ideas of the videos help us understand our answers to the first activity of the lesson?
- What goods that we currently buy/use can be associated with each of these two types of economic production/progress?

- **Commitment: A mosaic of ideas to bring about change in the future (25 mins)**
  - Students will work again in the same small groups from the beginning of the session. Together, they have to agree on a set of ideas or proposals that will help them contribute to challenge and bring about change to the current patterns of consumption and production (between 3 and 6 will work well). They will have to write them down in paper.
  - Questions that might help this activity are:
    - What can we do as consumers to reduce the impact of the products we buy on the sustainability of the planet?
    - What can we do as professionals (in our future jobs or occupations) to help reduce the amount of waste that is generated in the world?
    - What can we do as citizens to make sure that current and future generations are guaranteed life in a world with a clean and healthy environment?

  - Each group will read out loud their proposals and paste them in a wall or blackboard where everyone else can see them. The teacher can help facilitate the work by trying to group similar ideas and proposals in the same space.

  - To end the activity, the teacher or a student might share some closing remarks and reflections. If possible, photos of the mosaic with ideas and proposals for change can be taken and shared through social media.

Resources for students:
- Transitioning to a circular economy: http://tiny.cc/G12L4R5
- 5 Business Models that Put the Circular Economy to Work: http://tiny.cc/G12L4R6

- 7 Examples of Circular Economy: http://tiny.cc/G12L4R7

Resources for teachers:

- Global Dimension of Responsible Consumption and Production: http://tiny.cc/G12L4R8

Grade 12 Lesson 5

"Doing Good : Catalyzing local impact to make the world a better place"

Time Frame: 45 minutes, 3-5 sessions | **Subjects:** Current affairs, Government & Politics, Technology, Entrepreneurship
Designer: Heer Shaikh with Nicolás Riveros with Alexandra Ball, Deaweh Benson, Somoh Supharukchinda.

Standards: (SDG 10) Reduced Inequalities; (SDG 16) Peace, Justice, and Strong Institutions

Summary and Rationale:
Some of the most pressing socio-economic problems that the world is facing today, such as rising inequality, climate change and terrorism, to name a few, require the next generation to understand and tackle these issues from a multi-faceted approach. It is therefore imperative that not only do students graduating from school develop a deep understanding of the core issues that are fueling these crises, but are also equipped with the correct mindset and skill set to create localized solutions to these challenges. The first step would be to help the students gain a deeper understanding of their own strengths, passion and skills, which would allow them to craft a concrete path towards solving the issues that they feel the strongest about. It is also pertinent to instill in the students the realization that they cannot fix everything, and that progress in the real world is often defined by small, incremental steps towards a much larger goal that only comes to fruition in the long run. Thus, the students would be encouraged to think about novel solutions for problems that their local communities face, and how to scale the impact of these solutions.

Teachers are encouraged to redesign the lesson in whatever way better serves the context and particular characteristics of the students in their classes.

Instructional Goal: To use examples from current affairs, technology and politics to gain a deeper understanding of the most pressing issues that the world is facing, and develop local solutions for these problems

- ***Ethical and Intercultural Orientation (Feeling)***
  - o Cultivate a deep sense of compassion and empathy towards global and local crises and communities
  - o Understand the linkages between individuals, local communities, and global issues at large

- ***Knowledge and Skills (Thinking)***
  - o Understand the most pressing socio-economic issues that the world is facing, as well as the underlying reasons that cause these problems
  - o Recognise the unique skill set and mindset that needs to be cultivated for creating effective solutions to socio-economic challenges
  - o Analyze and research solutions to socio economic problems (income inequality, climate change, food security etc) from the perspectives of different stakeholders, such as end users, government, third party beneficiaries etc.

- ***Agency and Empowerment (Acting)***
  - o Create empowered students to create local change which contribute to a larger, global context (social change makers/ entrepreneurial leaders)

Understanding:

The long term solutions to the most pressing challenges that the world is currently facing need to be community-led, locally driven initiatives. These solutions holistically understand the underlying problems that the end users face, and ensure that the end result is a sustainable intervention that aims

Individuals have the ability to create long lasting and positive change in their local communities. However, cultivating change does not happen overnight, and is rather a long and arduous process. It is essential for the future generations to have a deep understanding of their own strengths and weaknesses, and the causes that they are passionate about. By properly aligning their fortes with their interests, it would be possible for the youth to collaborate and build up sustainable solutions for the problems that their local communities face.

Essential questions: How can individuals create local solutions to tackle global problems?

Student Learning Objectives (Students Will be Able To):
- The major headlining socio-economic problems that the world is facing in today's world are multi-faceted issues, whose underlying causes are often socio, economic and political in nature and political.
- Individuals have the ability to create long-lasting and positive change in their communities which contributes to a bigger picture.

Assessment: Students will be assessed on 1) their understanding and identification of a global issue and connecting it with their local realities, 2) their innovative approaches towards producing solutions to global problems.

Sequence of Activities:

- **Introduction (10 minutes)**
  Teacher asks students what are the most pressing issues in today's world.

- **Teacher draws a web of responses** on the board which shows how global and local problems are interconnected. **(5 minutes)**

- **Teacher gives a brief lecture** about the history of global crises and politics, and the current technological advancements used for alleviating global issues **(10 minutes)**

  For example, the teacher can give an example about how mobile technology is used to send immunization reminders to mothers in Kenya in order to ensure that mothers and their children are fully immunized.

- **Teacher leads discussion** on how the problem areas which were earlier identified by students can be tackled by technology. **(5 minutes)**

- **Students are divided into groups** based on topics of interest (similar interests are clustered together), and they collectively come up with an innovative solution to tackle the problem. **(15 minutes)**

- Each group shares what they decided. **(10 minutes)**

* In the following lessons, teachers can dedicate for more time for discussion and critique, and allow students to prototype their projects.

Resources for teachers and students:

- 80,000 hours - about using your career capital to create impact: http://tiny.cc/G12L5R1
- Effective altruism- how to effectively analyse issues that need to be addressed : http://tiny.cc/G12L5R2
- Dollar Street: http://tiny.cc/G12L5R3

Bios

Fernando M. Reimers is the Ford Foundation Professor of the Practice of International Education and Director of the Global Education Innovation Initiative and of the International Education Policy Master's Program at Harvard University.

Professor Reimers is an expert in the field of Global Education. His research and teaching focus on understanding how to educate children and youth so they can thrive in the 21st century. He studies how education policy and leadership foster educational innovation and quality improvement. As part of the work of the Global Education Innovation Initiative he leads, he and his colleagues conducted a comparative study of the goals of education as reflected in the curriculum in Chile, China, India, Mexico, Singapore and the United States, published as *Teaching and Learning for the 21st Century* by Harvard Education Press, a book which has also been published in Chinese, Portuguese and Spanish. A forthcoming book, also to be published by Harvard Education Press, studies programs around the world which support teachers in developing the professional competencies to teach holistically for the 21st Century.

A recent book, *Empowering Global Citizens,* is a complete K-12 curriculum of global citizenship education, which examines why global citizenship education, aligned with helping students advance human rights and contribute to the achievement of the Sustainable Development Goals is an imperative of our times. Two recently edited books compile the results of informed dialogues, designed to foster collective impact in the areas of teacher education in Massachusetts (*Fifteen Letters on Education in Singapore*) and in the area of Scaling 21st century education programs (*Empowering All Students at Scale*). A recent book, *One Student at a Time. Leading the Global Education Movement,* analyzes the crucial work of those who lead the expansion of educational opportunities for children and youth around the world.

He recently chaired a Global Alliance which produced a framework for collective impact in strengthening teacher preparation and support (*Connecting the Dots to build the future teaching and learning*). This report has been translated and published in Arabic, Portuguese and Spanish and used to steer national dialogues on how to create conditions to strengthen the teaching profession and improve the relevance of instruction.

Professor Reimers has worked to advance the contributions of colleges and universities to develop leadership that advances cosmopolitanism, democracy and economic and social innovation. He has led the development of several innovative programs at Harvard University, including the master's degree program in International Education Policy and various executive education programs, including a program to support education leaders working for UNICEF and a collaboration with the Universidad de Juiz de For a in Minas Gerais, Brazil, to develop a master's degree program in education leadership. He is a founding co-chair of the Advanced Leadership Initiative, a program which brings to the university outstanding individuals who have retired from a primary career and who are interested in devoting themselves to addressing significant social challenges. As chair of the Strategic Planning Committee of the Massachusetts Board of Higher Education he works with all public institutions of higher education in the State developing institutional strategies to enhance the relevance of their programs. He has advised a range of institutions of higher education on strategies to advance the global awareness of undergraduates and serves on the board of Laspau, a Harvard affiliated organization whose mission is to strengthen institutions of higher education in Latin America.

He has advanced the development of programs to provide students and recent college graduates opportunities to engage in service and to develop civic, global and leadership competencies through his service on the boards of numerous education organizations and foundations including Teach for All, World Teach, the Global Scholars Program at Bloomberg Philanthropies, Envoys, and the scholars advisory council of Facing History and Ourselves. He is a commissioner in the US Commission on UNESCO. In 2017 he received the Global Citizen Award from the Committee on Teaching about the United Nations for his work advancing global citizenship education. In 2015 he was appointed the C.J. Koh Visiting Professor of Education at the National Institute of Education in Singapore in recognition of his work in global education. He received an honorary doctorate from Emerson College for his work advancing human rights education. He is a Fellow of the International Academy of Education and a member of the Council of Foreign Relations.

Abimbola Adetunji is a drilling engineer who has hung up her boots to tackle the problem of education quality in Africa. Her Education experience includes creating curriculum for African children aged 0 - 6 for Tembo Education -- an education startup and volunteer work in Lagos Nigeria with an NGO -- Education Aid Initiative to improve the quality of education in partner public primary schools. She graduated from the International Education Policy Master's program at Harvard graduate school of education.

Alexandra Ball has a Masters of Education in International Education Policy at the Harvard Graduate School of Education. In her prior role as a Curriculum Writer for Bridge International Academies, Alexandra created over three terms of Science, Social Studies, and Health curriculum for academies in Uganda. Her background also includes: teaching in Cape Town, South Africa; developing curriculum for an international school in Ranomafana, Madagascar; and edited curricular materials for an early childhood-focused EdTech startup. Alexandra interned for Harvard Scholars at Risk, an organization that promotes academic freedom through specialized fellowships for persecuted scholars from around the world.

Christian Bautista is a veteran of the classroom as well as the private sector – while working full time for the past several years as a music educator, he has also served as a startup business leader and a full-stack software developer. More recently he has become involved as a policy consultant in education and international development for organizations such as UNESCO and WISE, and he has presented and consulted in contexts ranging from Boston to Cambodia to Australia. He has published work in several subfields of education including curriculum design, cognitive psychology, and leadership development.

Deaweh Benson graduated as the 2012 class valedictorian from Spelman College, and went on to work in classrooms in Shenzhen, China and literacy centers in Washington D.C. She completed a Master's in the Harvard International Education Policy program, focusing on higher education strategies to prepare students to interact across difference.

Nicolás Buchbinder has a Master's of Education in International Education Policy at the Harvard Graduate School of Education and holds a degree in Education Sciences from the University of Buenos Aires. Nicolás has worked in teacher training and education policy research in Argentina, and has also taught at the undergraduate level.

Isabelle Byusa has a Master's of Education in International Education Policy at the Harvard Graduate School of Education. Isabelle's experience includes creating an year-long entrepreneurship curriculum for secondary school students in Rwanda, a toolkit to support entrepreneurship educators through innovative activities in the classroom, and curating content for ABLConnect, an online repository for activity-based learning at the Derek Bok Center for Teaching and Learning.

Wendi Cui has a Master's of Education in International Education Policy at Harvard Graduate School of Education. Wendi has a strong passion for providing quality education to children in developing regions through teacher development and school reforms. She used to work with FAROF in Nigeria to design projects on ICT literacy building and girls' education. Later she served as a program assistant for UNESCO-IICBA, doing policy analysis on ICT integration and teacher capacity building in SSA countries.

Elaine Ding has a Master's of Education in International Education Policy at the Harvard Graduate School of Education. Her areas of interest include: education in emergencies, girls' education, global citizenship education, and child protection. Elaine has worked with vulnerable communities for over 8 years in both domestic and international contexts. She was a former prison GED tutor, refugee English teacher, women's shelter volunteer coordinator, and primary school teacher. Elaine holds a B.S.F.S. from Georgetown University.

Madhuri Dhariwal is a teacher and aspiring policy maker. She has taught in India – in Mumbai, with the Akanksha Foundation and in Raipur, C.G., at a night shelter program in collaboration with the Indian government. She is extremely passionate about- teacher education, out-of-school education and adult learning. She is also researching ways in which both data analysis and technology can be used to make education practice and research better. In Boston, she is currently working with HarvardX, co-creating content for an online course on data analysis. She holds a B.Ed. degree from PRSU, India and an Ed.M. in International Education Policy, from the Harvard Graduate School of Education.

Cassie Fuenmayor has a Master's of Education in International Education Policy. She has experience teaching in public schools as well as working as the Lead Teacher for the Bridge2Rwanda Scholars Program. In Rwanda, she designed a curriculum to help prepare Rwandan students for higher education content abroad. She is currently working as an Educational Advisor for a start up in Liberia, preparing a curriculum that combines college preparatory content with ideas of global citizenship.

Kara Howard has a Master's of Education in International Education Policy from the Harvard Graduate School of Education. She served as primary English teacher and teacher trainer as a Peace Corps volunteer in Lesotho from 2013-2015. She has also taught middle school in Khayelitsha, South Africa and Puriscal, Costa Rica. Before working abroad she served as a Jumpstart AmeriCorps member and worked in bilingual elementary school in Washington, D.C.. She is currently the Teacher Quality Program Manager at WorldTeach, working to redesign their professional development program to incorporate best practices in teaching and 21st Century Skill development in students.

Heather Kesselman has a Master's of Education in International Education Policy from the Harvard Graduate School of Education. She taught math, history, and special education in New York City for several years, and holds a Master's of Education in Literacy. She has also worked on curriculum design for a progressive school in Madagascar, refugee camps in Greece and Jordan, and charter schools in Brooklyn, New York.

Katherine Kinnaird has a Master's of Education in International Education Policy from the Harvard Graduate School of Education. She also holds a Master's in Religion in Women's, Gender, and Sexuality Studies from Yale University and has teaching experience ranging from a women's empowerment center in Morocco to an all-girls school in Amman, Jordan. In addition to her work in Morocco and Jordan, she has worked in refugee camps throughout Greece developing non-formal learning opportunities for Syrian, Iraqi, and Afghan children.

Maria Lee has a Master's of Education candidate in Human Development and Psychology from the Harvard Graduate School of Education. She has previously worked as a teacher's assistant in a kindergarten and first grade classroom in Ithaca, NY. She is also a former lab manager at Cornell Early Childhood Cognition Lab, where she worked with 3-4 year-old children to study how they explore their physical and social worlds.

Sharon Jiae Lee has a strong passion for empowering low-income students through language education. She taught English to middle school and high school students in Mexico and South Korea before founding an edtech startup called LightedEd that offered high quality of English education at an affordable cost. She has Master's in Education in International Education Policy Program from Harvard Graduate School of Education.

Quinn Lockwood has a Master's of Education from the Harvard Graduate School of Education. She has a background in international studies and has worked most recently as an early childhood educator and curriculum designer in Hong Kong. Quinn is currently working on intergenerational programming designed to bring senior citizens and children together for mutual benefit.

Eva Flavia Martínez Orbegozo has a Master's of Education in Education Policy and Management from the Harvard Graduate School of Education and holds degrees in Architecture and English Language and Literature. She was a fellow in the second cohort of Empieza Por Educar, part of the Teach For All network in Spain, and remained as a Math, English, Art, Technology and Science teacher for two more years after the fellowship. During this time Eva Flavia worked at Padre Piquer, an ASHOKA Changemaker school, and was part of the team leading the expansion of their innovative Multi-task Collaborative Classroom model.

Xin Miao has a Masters of Education in International Education Policy from the Harvard Graduate School of Education. Prior to HGSE, she worked at an elite high school in Guangzhou for almost 4 years. With extensive teaching and management experience in Chinese schools, she knows how the basic education system in the country works. She believes that effective reform and investment in education should focus on improving the learning experience and learning outcome of every child. Her interest lies in researching and expanding personalized learning programs that work across contexts.

Matthew Owens has a Master's of Education in International Education Policy from the Harvard Graduate School of Education. Matt has served as an English and Social Sciences teacher with the Fulbright Commission in Spain, where he worked with the regional government to organize and teach the Global Classrooms project, a global citizenship initiative designed to empower students to achieve the Millennium Development Goals. Matt currently works for WorldTeach creating teacher professional development modules for volunteer teachers and for Two Rabbits, where he is designing a curricular framework for the organization's education in conflict standards.

Theodosia Papazis has a Masters of Education in International Education Policy from the Harvard Graduate School of Education. She served as a teacher for seven years and an instructional leader in Denver, Colorado at a high school that specialized in refugee and English Language Acquisition services. She served as a supervising practitioner for the Teacher Education Program at HGSE and is on a team that is building an NGO that will coordinate to women and children in Greece.

Arianna Pattek has a Master's of Education in International Education Policy from the Harvard Graduate School of Education. She is a returned Peace Corps Volunteer, serving in Madagascar from 2012 until 2015. In Madagascar, she taught *6ème* and *1ère* English classes and developed teacher training curricula. She also has fieldwork experience in Kenya and Tanzania. Currently, she is the Director of Student Consultants for the Ranomafana International School in Madagascar, overseeing the development of a curriculum that incorporates 21st century skills relevant to the Malagasy context.

Emily Pope has worked in curriculum development and delivery for over six years. She has taught in Turkey with the Turkish Fulbright Commission and in New York City with the International Rescue Committee. Currently, she works on blended learning, global education programs at Harvard Medical School. Emily is passionate about leveraging technology to enhance curriculum delivery and to reach a global student population. Emily holds an Ed. M. in International Education Policy from Harvard Graduate School of Education and a B.A. in International Development and Philosophy from Calvin College.

Vijayaragavan Prabakaran, an engineer turned educator, has a Masters of Education in International Education Policy from the Harvard Graduate School of Education. Previously, he was a Teach for India Fellow, and taught grades 2 and 3 in a public school in Chennai, India, serving a low income muslim community. He created several elementary grade literacy and numeracy instructional materials and classroom culture aids that were used by teachers across 7 cities in India. Recently, he worked with UNESCO, researching on the area of 'Teacher Motivation' towards achieving the SDG4.

Nicolás Riveros is a Masters in Political Science from Universidad de los Andes, Colombia. He worked for 6 years in Fe y Alegría, a popular education movement serving underprivileged communities in Latin

America. As a program coordinator, he served schools and education leaders in Argentina, Brasil, Colombia, Chile, El Salvador, Guatemala, Panama and Peru. He also was part of a team that developed curriculum materials for civic education for the Secretary of Education of Bogotá in 2014. He completed a Master's of Education in International Education Policy at the Harvard Graduate School of Education.

Ben Searle has a Master's of Education in International Education Policy from the Harvard Graduate School of Education. He is a returned Peace Corps volunteer and the co-founder of Ultimate Without Borders, a sport for development organization based in Panama. While working in Panama, Ben developed a comprehensive reproductive health curriculum that has been used throughout the country.

Tatiana Shevchenko believes that young people should do work they love with organizations they admire. To further this mission she leads a youth employment organization, www.adastragroup.org, in the Republic of Moldova. Though Ad Astra, Tatiana has conducted national and international-scale youth employment projects in partnership with USAID, The Council of Europe, The German Federal Foreign Ministry, the Ministry of Education of the Republic of Moldova among others. Tatiana leads projects that connect and prepare youth for the creative industries sector, vocational education, and entrepreneurship. In Boston, Tatiana is a Teaching Fellow at the Harvard Graduate School of Education, she conducts research on work-based learning at "Jobs for the Future," and develops content for mass open online courses at "HarvardX". Tatiana is interested in youth labor migration, technological unemployment, and the future of work.

Heer Shaikh has a Masters of Education in International Education Policy from the Harvard Graduate School of Education. Prior to her Master's candidacy, she worked with the Secretary of Education in Sindh, Pakistan on enhancing the governance and accountability of public education stakeholders (mainly teachers and district leaders), and was also part of the team that drafted the first early childhood policy of the state. She has taught English to students in an urban-slum in Karachi, Pakistan and Gaziantep, Turkey.

Sam (Shiv) Sharma has a Master's of Education in International Education Policy from the Harvard Graduate School of Education. Sam is deeply interested in exploring the nexus between entrepreneurship and education. Sam founded The Northwood Program, a global education "learning through travel" program. Last year Sam established a "Community Classroom" in a Delhi slum for underprivileged and marginalized children. He founded "Global Educators" a student organization at Harvard Graduate School of Education whose mission is promoting global education at Harvard University and elsewhere. He also organized and led the first Harvard India Study Trek this March. Sam also produced an independent movie "Just Indian" (2005) while living in New York city.

Chloé Suberville has a masters of education in International Education Policy from the Harvard Graduate School of Education. She is passionate about global citizenship, empathy and equity in schools. Previously, Chloé was a classroom teacher in Orangeburg, South Carolina where she taught Spanish and organized travel opportunities for her students. She has engaged with education in different milieus, including in the humanitarian and micro-finance fields. She has worked in Haïti, Nicaragua, Mexico and the United States.

Somoh Supharukchinda has an M.Ed. in International Education Policy at the Harvard Graduate School of Education. Previously, Somoh worked as the Director of Growth Strategy & Development Communications for Teach For All, a non-profit that aims to cultivate the leadership to expand educational opportunity. Somoh also brings experience from the Colorado and New York City Departments of Education, where she supported district/school data analysis and improvement planning efforts, and the JUMP! Foundation, where she co-developed curriculum and programming for a leadership summit for secondary students across Africa.

Corrie Sutherland has a Masters of Education in International Education Policy from the Harvard Graduate School of Education. Corrie's prior experience includes being a program associate with InsidenGO in Washington, D.C. and a High School English Language Arts teacher for two years in Charlotte, North Carolina. She has worked in Hong Kong, Philippines, Swaziland, Indonesia, Vietnam, Cambodia, and Thailand. Corrie is passionate about the power of education and international development relief work in South East Asia.

Tisha Verma holds a BA(Hons) in English Language and Literature from the University of Oxford and an MA in Arts in Leadership from UCL, with a dissertation focus on gender stereotyping in Mumbai classrooms. She has a Masters of Education in International Education Policy from the Harvard

Graduate School of Education. She has worked as a teacher and education consultant in London, Beijing and the UAE over the past seven years.

Devon Wilson has over 10 years of experience working with educational projects in the US and China. Devon is currently working as a Project Coordinator and Research Assistant for the Interdisciplinary and Global Studies Project at Project Zero, Harvard Graduate School of Education, where he assists in teacher training and conducts research on US-China blended pedagogical approaches and best practices in global competence education. His prior experience includes serving as a Teaching Fellow and Curriculum Writer at Teach for China (美丽中国); studying education with the Fulbright program at Shaanxi Normal University in Xi'an, China; and serving as a program manager for a young entrepreneur non-profit at UC Berkeley. Devon is passionate about helping students develop a love of learning; giving students opportunities to learn in deep and meaningful ways; and creating cross cultural learning opportunities for students.

Holing Yip has a Master's of Education in Education Policy and Management from the Harvard Graduate School of Education. She previously worked in education policy advocacy and research for a non-profit advocating for racial equity in Hong Kong, and focused on Chinese as a second language policy and racial integration in schools. Her teaching and curriculum experience includes teaching third-grade social studies in New York City, and teaching at Summerbridge in Hong Kong, a summer program for eighth- and ninth-grade students from low-income backgrounds.

Chihiro Yoshida has a Master's of Education in International Education Policy from the Harvard Graduate School of Education. Her passion towards intercultural education stems from the two years she spent in rural India as a high school student, where she developed lessons plans to teach English and Math to 7th grade students. She worked as an economic consultant in the private sector for three years before pursuing her Master's degree.